LESSONS FOR LIFE

Career Development Activities Library

Volume 2: Secondary Grades

Zark VanZandt

Bette Ann Buchan

Illustrations by Eileen Ciavarella

*The Center for Applied
Research in Education
West Nyack, NY 10994*

Library of Congress Cataloging-in-Publication Data

VanZandt, Zark.
    Lessons for life : a complete career development curriculum for busy educators / Zark
VanZandt, Bettie Ann Buchan.
      p. cm.
    Includes bibliographical references.
    Contents: v 2. Elementary level
    ISBN 0-87628-515-9
    1. Student aspirations. 2. Educational counseling. 3. Vocational guidance. 4. Career
education. 5. Life skills. I. VanZandt, Zark. II. Title
LB1027.8B83 1997
372.14'2—dc21   97-28088
                                                                                CIP

Printed in the United States of America

10 9 8 7 6 5 4 3 2 1

ISBN 0-87628-515-9 (Spiral)

ATTENTION: CORPORATIONS AND SCHOOLS

The Center for Applied Research in Education books are available at
quantity discounts with bulk purchase for educational, business, or
sales promotional use. For information, please write to: Prentice Hall
Career & Personal Development Special Sales, 240 Frisch Court,
Paramus, NJ 07652. Please supply: title of book, ISBN number, quantity,
how the book will be used, date needed.

**THE CENTER FOR APPLIED RESEARCH
IN EDUCATION**
West Nyack, NY 10994
A Simon & Schuster Company

On the World Wide Web at http://www.phdirect.com

Prentice-Hall International (UK) Limited, *London*
Prentice-Hall of Australia Pty. Limited, *Sydney*
Prentice-Hall Canada, Inc., *Toronto*
Prentice-Hall Hispanoamericana, S.A., *Mexico*
Prentice-Hall of India Private Limited, *New Delhi*
Prentice-Hall of Japan, Inc., *Tokyo*
Simon & Schuster Asia Pte. Ltd., *Singapore*
Editora Prentice-Hall do Brasil, Ltda., *Rio de Janeiro*

About the Authors

Zark VanZandt is a counselor educator at the University of Southern Maine in Gorham. In the earlier part of his career journey, he was both an elementary and a high school counselor, a Director of Guidance, a state guidance consultant, and a counselor educator in two other states. Zark has presented workshops at the national, regional, and state levels, and has written articles for several journals and newsletters. Zark and Bette Ann previously collaborated on a Public Relations kit for the American School Counselor Association. His most recent professional activities have included his role as the project consultant for ASCA's *Get a Life* portfolio and as the coauthor of a textbook on comprehensive developmental school counseling programs. Zark received his B.A. and M.A. degrees from Michigan State University and his doctorate from the University of Maine. He resides in Gorham with his wife and three sons.

Bette Ann Buchan is an elementary/middle school counselor at Woolwich Central School, Woolwich, Maine, where she initiated and now implements a comprehensive K-8 guidance program. She came to that position with teaching experience ranging from kindergarten to adult. Outside the school setting, she consults for UNUM America in their Career Development and Resource Center and is an adjunct clinical supervisor for interns at the University of Southern Maine Counselor Education program. Bette Ann has presented workshops at the state, regional, and local levels on topics ranging from integrating music into classroom guidance lessons to public relations. She received her B.A. degree from St. Joseph's College in North Windham, Maine, and her M.Ed. in guidance and counseling from University of Central Oklahoma in Edmond. She resides in the town of Woolwich with her husband and two college-age children.

How to Use *Lessons for Life*

The activities in *Lessons for Life* were written by and for busy educators; written for teachers and counselors who want to lay their hands on a self-contained resource that has clear skill-based objectives, accessible supplies and available worksheets, a high-interest age-appropriate lesson design, and measurable outcomes. Those criteria were foundational to the creation of the lessons in this book.

Chapters 4 through 7 are organized according to the same categories used in the American School Counselor Association's *Get a Life* portfolio. As we mention elsewhere in the book, you do not have to be using the *Get a Life* portfolio to use and benefit from the lessons in this book. The four categories of Self-Knowledge, Life Roles, Educational Development, and Career Exploration and Planning are foundational components of almost any "good" career guidance program.

Each of the four chapters devoted to lesson plans has been divided into five subheadings, each containing three lessons. You now have 60 lessons (120 in the two-volume set) to aid students in the reflective process of examining who they are, how their life roles have developed, the relevance of their education, and the significant factors that contribute to positive career choices.

Most lessons can be completed in one 40-minute session. However, some "continued" lessons need additional time for such things as independent student research, written assignments, and interviews. Many lessons also have suggested follow-up activities; thus, facilitators are encouraged to extend the lessons with the suggested ideas or your own original ideas that might capitalize on the students' processing statements during the lesson's closure.

Reproducible worksheets have been developed for certain lessons. Other supplies commonly found in schools may also be needed (e.g., chart paper, markers) or may be readily available from students' homes. Some lessons may require resource materials found in the library or guidance and counseling office.

Each complete lesson is organized on two facing pages. The left sheet we refer to as the "Preview Page," where we list the lesson title, the career topic being addressed, the skill-based objectives, supplies needed, and an indication of where students' reflections about the lesson might be entered if you are using the *Get a Life* portfolio. It is suggested that the person facilitating the lesson spend at least a little time reviewing the objectives and organizing the supplies. Particular classes, because of students' unique learning needs or the significance of the topic, may require special accommodations, and a quick preview will help the facilitator be attentive to those needs.

The objectives of the lessons are skill-based, indicating what the students will know or be able to do after the lesson is completed. Two simple evaluation/feedback sheets are provided in the Epilogue section of this book to assist you in determining whether the objectives have been met. It may not be necessary to use such an assessment for every lesson, but the results of simple formative evaluations such as these can be helpful for suggesting changes or highlighting major successes. They can also be used as simple tools for promoting accountability in the delivery of the career development curriculum.

On the facing page is the actual lesson, including the Introduction, Focus, Activity, Closure, and sometimes a suggestion for a Follow-up Activity. A "Notes" section is also provided on this page so the person facilitating the lesson may make personal comments for additions or deletions to the lesson. This space for notes is a good place to make accommodations in the lessons and to record the insights and ideas that are a result of your own reflective practice. In the future, being prepared for changes in the lesson will contribute to the ease with which the instructor delivers the lesson and the students grasp the significance of the lesson.

The special ingredient that makes any lesson better is the enthusiasm of the facilitator, and it is often the critical factor in the lesson's success. With the continued use of the resources in *Lessons for Life,* and with the refinements you make in the "Notes" section of the lessons, you should be able to infuse your own enthusiasm in their delivery by noting the way the lessons complement your own career development journey, your personality and style, and the goals you have set for the curriculum's success. Because we are role models for young people as they make meaning of their lives and begin their own journeys and searches for careers that matter, our enthusiasm for that process will make a significant statement about how we value our students as individuals. Enjoy the journey.

Zark VanZandt
Bette Ann Buchan

"Life's Journey" as Metaphor

As we have reflected on the essence of this practical collection of resources for busy educators, we have felt a need to reiterate two important themes that have guided our efforts and defined our mission. The first theme is that of "career as life"; the second depicts career as a life journey.

All too often, *career* is seen as one's occupation or sequence of jobs. The perspective we want to promote—and it is reinforced by many Career Development scholars—is that one's career is an integration of several very important life roles. Our choices about how we balance the roles of family member, leisurite, citizen, spiritual being, friend, *and* worker will define the measure of our career success. Individuals must seek their own balance that fits their unique circumstances, and in creating that balance, their lives become more fulfilling. This is a lesson that needs to be taught early and often in the schools.

Obviously, the roles stated above will not remain stagnant, but will change according to an individual's circumstances, age, and personal life history. For example, the role of family member may be more prominent when a child is dependent on a parent—or vice versa. At other times in a person's life, a spiritual peace may take on greater emphasis and meaning, for a variety of reasons. Students in graduate school often lament the absence of leisure activities in their lives. As schools help students understand these interdependent roles, they can be instrumental in providing the knowledge and skills to cope with life's passages and changes. If one's career is seen as one's life, not one's job, then the individual can begin to see that life is a process of understanding and making a commitment to the balancing of multiple life roles.

The ever-changing realities of life take each of us on a unique and fascinating journey through various highways, side trips, peaks and valleys, tourist traps, and major attractions. We subscribe to the notion that one's journey through life (career) can be a well-planned trip or a random series of adventures or detours. Schools that are trying to empower youth to take control of their futures are aligned with the former metaphor instead of the latter. In *Lessons for Life,* we introduce each chapter with a subtitle that highlights a different part of the career/life journey. Students may need assistance in understanding some of the subtleties and nuances of this metaphor as they participate in the lessons in this book, but the insight into their personal life journey may be one of the most important lessons they will learn during their school years. Well-planned career journeys should help them make sense of their current educational experiences, while assisting them as they focus on their futures.

Obviously, the use of metaphors is not unique to this book. The use of the journey metaphor provides one example of how the *Lessons for Life* curriculum is an *integrated* curriculum. Metaphors can be used in language arts and history classrooms with very little disruption to the normal routine. Many of the lessons in this book could easily be infused in other content areas, as well. For a developmental life skills curriculum to be truly successful, it must be comprehensive—and to be truly comprehensive, we recommend that it be integrated into the regular academic curriculum.

We hope you, too, enjoy your journey through the pages of *Lessons for Life,* especially as you venture out into some of the lesson plans that have been "mapped out" for your use. Keep your eyes on the horizon, as well as the compass, and may all your passengers be happy travelers.

Acknowledgments

We have worked together on a number of projects since 1987, and both have felt compelled to respond to the need for a comprehensive career curriculum that was practical and user-friendly. Writing this book was lots of fun, though. In fact, people would sometimes comment that we seemed to be having too much fun to be writing a book. Along the way, we became increasingly excited as family, colleagues, and students nurtured our efforts.

Bette Ann's husband, Ian, and son, Ian, provided long-standing support and understanding as a myriad of papers covered every flat surface in the house. Daughter Jennifer became integrally involved as the designer of many worksheets and most important as a continual cheerleader (cards, letters, and phone calls greatly appreciated!).

Administrators, staff, and students (including USM interns) at Woolwich Central School who, because of their high standards and high expectations, insisted upon a well-designed, skill-based, practical program will recognize most of the Lessons for Life. Their suggestions for each lesson greatly enhanced their creation and Bette Ann's role as a school counselor.

Zark's wife, Kitty, is a director of guidance, as well as a high school counselor, and has provided a valuable perspective about the challenges facing teenagers. Sons Tygh, Tod, and Kyle provide a reality base for thinking about the important lessons that need to be included across a broad age range to prepare students for an ever-changing world of work. All four have recognized Zark's need for such creative outlets and have provided much appreciated support and encouragement for this project.

Zark's school counseling students and professional colleagues at USM have been a constant source of ideas, motivation, and resourcefulness. It is inspirational to share in the vision and the challenge of creating quality career curriculum materials that our students can use to empower youth. Their excitement about their chosen profession is infectious. As they have graduated from the program, many students have asked, "When can I get my hands on that book you've been working on?" What really makes creative scholarship such an enjoyable part of Zark's work at the University of Southern Maine is being a part of a counselor education program that is second to none, a department that is "the best," a College of Education and Human Development that operates according to a best practices mentality, and a university that acknowledges as one of its core values a commitment to linking theory to practice.

A special thank you goes to Kerry Bertalan, who has patiently abided our frenzied styles and has meticulously typed, organized, edited, and refined the manuscript, especially in its final stages. We are truly blessed to have her be a part of this effort. She's one in a million!

We also want to acknowledge the creative talents of Wendy Rudolph, who created the cartoon in the Step-by-Step lesson in the elementary volume.

We would like to thank the following reviewers for their helpful comments and suggestions, which were especially useful in shaping the final product:

Finally, we would like to acknowledge the support and guidance of Susan Kolwicz, our Acquisitions Editor at the Center for Applied Research in Education, who has always been responsive to our questions, concerns, and anxieties. It was reassuring to work with an editor who listened to the needs of the authors while also attending to the requisite demands of the publishing company.

Our ultimate acknowledgment is to both present and future generations of students. We firmly believe in the adage that children are our future; it is what inspires us to go to work every day and to work on projects like *Lessons for Life*.

Contents

CHAPTER FOUR
In the Driver's Seat
Lessons to Promote Self-Knowledge
27

CHAPTER FIVE
Nice Set o' Wheels
Lessons to Help Students Examine Life Roles
75

CHAPTER SIX
Start Your Engines
Lessons to Promote Educational Development
127

CHAPTER SEVEN
The Road Map
Lessons to Foster Career Exploration and Planning
177

EPILOGUE
A Look in the Rearview Mirror
Reflections on *Lessons for Life*
225

CHAPTER ONE

Two Roads Diverged...

A Focus for the *Lessons for Life* Curriculum

In the following scenario, you are witness to a telephone conversation between two high school seniors (stay with us, elementary and middle school folks; there's a message here for you, as well):

Hi, Kim. I'm glad I caught you before you went to work. You'll never guess who I met while shopping at the mall—Mike Taylor! I hadn't seen him since his family moved to Hicksville in sixth grade. He's just as nice as he was back then, and he suggested we catch up on things over a pizza.

When I told him I was shopping for clothes, he said, "Yah, like who has money for clothes these days?!" So, of course I told him how I had fallen into the best part-time job while interviewing an accountant for my portfolio activity. He got this strange look on his face and said, "Portfolio? What's that?"

Can you imagine? He had no idea that we'd been working on our career portfolios since about the time he moved six years ago. Weren't we working on them when he was there? Anyway, I told him that over the years, we had been making entries in our portfolios, so that when it came time to make our first real career decisions, we'd have all this great information to draw on ... and now it was really starting to pay off.

You know what he said? "Boy, I wouldn't know where to start." That's pretty sad. So, I told him about all the cooperative learning activities, guest speakers from the community, interviews, family research projects, interest inventories, role plays, and all. He just couldn't believe it.

Remember that assignment we had where we had to write a letter to our unborn child telling about ourselves and our dreams for the baby's future? I told him about that, and he said, "Man, I don't have the foggiest idea about my own future. I've just taken the minimum requirements for graduation and played sports. Football is the only thing I'm really good at, so I'll probably try out for a pro team someday."

You know, Kim, he's a real nice guy, but I'm not sure he has a clue about where he's going and how he's going to get there. I guess with all the stuff we've been exposed to, we seem to have some lessons about life that he's really missed out on."

This scenario could happen in "Anytown," as students who have participated in developmental career guidance programs speak to peers who haven't. Educators have a significant responsibility to assist students in analyzing and synthesizing information about their lives that will lead to more purposeful and meaningful careers.

As the scenario suggests, laying the foundation for such important life decisions takes *years* of development and nurturing. Critical skills need to be taught, concepts explored, and options evaluated. The challenge we face as educators is to put these important learning opportunities into some kind of understandable sequence of lessons that will help students grasp their significance and then begin to make the process work for them.

Another chore for busy educators, you say? No, not really. What the above scenario does suggest, more than anything else, is that students really need a career guidance *curriculum—a conceptual framework*—that helps them do the investigating, reflecting, analyzing, and synthesizing so they can see how this interconnected puzzle of school and job and life fits together. You are probably already providing some of these important lessons in your classrooms and group activities. What *Lessons for Life* does is to offer educators a time-efficient resource that addresses the four major competency areas needed for successful life skills and career development—and it provides that conceptual framework that students so desperately need. The addition of *Lessons for Life* to your instructional materials will just complement, "spice up," and give a better context to the excellent things you are already doing.

School counselors often use the term "developmental" to explain the perspective of the guidance and counseling program, to help understand students' needs and behavior at different ages, and to appreciate the progressive nature of the educational process as we work with individuals and groups over several years while they are in school. Our own professional growth as educators is also best represented in a developmental perspective. Just as we do not expect students to be fully empowered to handle life's adjustments, neither can we expect new counselors and teachers to begin their careers with a fully integrated career development curriculum that totally reflects their unique talents and skills. Actually, we don't even have such expectations for "experienced" educators, since the concept of a developmental career guidance curriculum may be new to them, as well. As the metaphor suggests, the curriculum road has diverged in recent years, and a great deal more emphasis is being placed on how schools prepare youth for school-to-work transitions. At the same time, each educator approaches that fork in the road from a developmental perspective that represents her or his unique training, personality, and experience. As teachers and community members become more involved in this career development journey, we must be sensitive to where these people are developmentally, as well. This book of lessons was designed with the career development *program* in mind—while also attending to both the issues of the students who must make those difficult choices about their lives and the educators who will play such critical roles in those decisions. Practitioners are encouraged to use the book and apply its lessons according to their own professional stage of development, constantly striving to nurture their skills and expertise as providers of a quality career guidance curriculum.

Lessons for Life was initially created in response to scores of requests from counselors, teachers, and administrators throughout the United States (and even some foreign countries) who wanted one set of "lessons" that could accompany the *Get a Life* Personal Planning Portfolio, a resource that was cooperatively developed by the American School Counselor Association and the National Occupational Information Coordinating Committee (NOICC). However, it became very apparent in the early stages of development that *Lessons for Life* was going to be equally valuable for counselors and teachers who were not using *Get a Life*. Essentially, it is a resource for educators who embrace the value and significance of a developmental curriculum that focuses on the essential lessons that students need to make good personal, social, educational, and career decisions in their lives.

The *Get a Life* portfolio was created as a prototype model for managing and delivering a comprehensive developmental career guidance program. Because the model recognizes that excellent lessons and practices are already in operation in most schools, it provides a flexible framework for integrating a variety of useful strategies and resources. However, many educators—especially those in the early developmental stages of creating a career development curriculum—expressed frustration at having to draw upon a whole array of resources to address students' self-knowledge, life role understanding, educational development, and career exploration and planning needs. The task just seemed too complex and demanding. *Lessons for Life* started out as a resource for those people who had been saying, "Give me *one* good resource that will help me see how to make this all work!"

Schools know they should have a career guidance curriculum, but who has the time to create one? This book provides the framework and the lessons to assist school counselors, teachers, and other educators as they embark upon the tremendous challenge of creating a career development curriculum that is focused, flexible, and fun.

Lessons for Life is definitely *focused*. It is focused on a comprehensive developmental career guidance program model, while providing separate volumes of lessons at the elementary and secondary school levels. When used accordingly, it can be focused on the topical framework used in the *Get a Life* Portfolio, thus creating many opportunities for student reflection and "best work" contributions to their life planning. It is also focused on the National Career Development Guidelines (as was the *Get a Life* Portfolio) as a source of content validity. The Guidelines are a nationally validated life-span model of career development, and they provide a well-developed list of competencies that individuals should possess to be successful in a competitive world economy. Essentially, the Guidelines help students focus on the divergent paths they can choose so they make their decisions with their eyes open.

We have also designed *Lessons for Life* to be *flexible*. Several design features acknowledge the importance of educators adding their own creative touches and addressing the unique needs of the school or community. The format of the lessons allows you to add your own ideas and resources. As your program needs change, your curriculum should reflect those changes, so you can refine both the content and the mode of instruction. The comprehensive categories for the lessons provide you with a contextual framework you can use for classifying other lessons you have created to meet the unique needs of your school or classroom. The Notes section on each lesson plan is offered as a place where you can write your own suggestions for improving or changing a lesson—or for writing reminders about important points to make in the lesson.

You will also note that some of the lessons provide flexibility for creating advanced learning opportunities and extensions of the lessons. Most lessons can be conducted within a typical class period; however, some may be adapted as career guidance units or be extended through homework assignments and community projects. Finally, the lessons are flexible in promoting an integrated curriculum. Teachers in a variety of disciplines will be able to see how the lessons complement their classes' subject matter.

Being focused and flexible is certainly important, but we really wanted the *Lessons for Life* to be *fun*. Students will enjoy the creative strategies for discovering their personal strengths, challenges, influences, interests, goals, and opportunities. Even the names of the lessons can be fun for students as they try to figure out why a lesson on self-concept is called "Pass the Roles" or why "Power of the Stars" is the name of a lesson on job-seeking skills. All the lessons try to actively engage students in their own developmental process. The message on the back cover of the *Get a Life* portfolio encourages students to "enjoy a wonderful journey of exploration as you discover who you are and what you want for your future." If they are to enjoy the journey and know the right way to go when the roads diverge, students need to know that much of the reflective and decision-making process can be fun, too.

We hope that your Career Development Curriculum is full of lessons for life. As you develop a curriculum that assists youth in developing the knowledge, skills, and attributes that will empower them in a complex world, we also hope that *Lessons for Life* helps to empower you.

Students talk about their school experiences well after graduation. Students who use *Lessons for Life* will be able to compare notes with those students who attended schools that didn't use such lessons and say that they were able to choose "the road less traveled … and that has made all the difference."

CHAPTER TWO

The Lay of the Land

A Foundation for Understanding *Lessons for Life*

Lessons for Life was designed to focus on practical ideas you can use in classrooms to empower students to make good choices in their lives. However, practical ideas work best when used in the context of a larger framework that provides depth and meaning to those ideas. Continuing the metaphor that one's career is a journey through life, this chapter helps you, the educator, to be a better tour guide by understanding the "lay of the land."

We hesitate to use the word, because we know that some people find this part of a resource to be less exciting and creative than the lessons, but here goes, anyway. This chapter is about theory and philosophy. Now, we realize that you may be tempted to avoid the "theoretical stuff" and turn directly to the lesson plans, but we want to encourage you to resist that temptation so we can share some information that will provide the contextual framework for maximizing those lesson plans. This chapter and the following chapter of practical suggestions provide the larger picture into which these lessons fit. The best tour guides know how to enrich a journey with the special knowledge and insight they have about "what's out there" and what people need or want to know. Educators helping students on their career journeys need to provide similar insights.

School-aged students are already in the midst of their own career development, although too often it seems more like haphazard wandering than a trip with a clear destination. Acknowledging that career development is a process, not an event, schools must nurture that development from the first day of kindergarten—when we open children's eyes to the possibilities before them—until students graduate from high school—when they should be focused and excited about embarking upon their future choices and development. To get to this focused time in their lives, students need to be nurtured through stages of awareness, exploration, decision making, and planning. The whole community needs to be involved in students' career development, but the schools must create the structure and the opportunities for aspirations to be realized. The career guidance curriculum is the most feasible means of providing that integrated structure and those opportunities. Since the career guidance curriculum cuts across disciplines and grade levels, students begin to see the interconnectedness of their school experience—the lay of the land.

In the following sections, we are going to share some of the theoretical and philosophical perspectives that undergird a comprehensive career guidance curriculum. These are separate but related paradigms that, when brought together, provide a powerful synergistic model of empowerment for youth. The comprehensive developmental guidance and counseling model is explained because it offers a holistic framework that complements the *Lessons for Life* and *Get a Life* delivery systems. In fact, in some schools, counselors may be the sole proprietors of the comprehensive career guidance curriculum.

Three other broad-based initiatives are also summarized. The National Career Development Guidelines and the SCANS (Secretary's Commission on Achieving Necessary Skills) Competencies are both national models of excellence that were created with all educators in mind—administrators, teachers, counselors, and members of the community. Career development facilitators who want to understand the lay of the land should know something about these significant initiatives, so that future plans and actions are in keeping with the vision of our national leaders.

The last section shares information about the authentic assessment movement, which is a major topic in school reform discussions. The reflective learning model encourages students to take more ownership of their educational experiences. This concept has significance in that *Lessons for Life* provides opportunities for students to assume more ownership of their own life journeys.

COMPREHENSIVE DEVELOPMENTAL GUIDANCE AND COUNSELING PROGRAMS

For more than two decades, leaders in school counseling have been advocating a comprehensive developmental model, with the concept gaining more refinement and definition as it has matured. While reasons exist why schools have not embraced and implemented comprehensive developmental school counseling and guidance programs, there are no excuses. The following foundational explanation will highlight basic elements of a comprehensive developmental program, but you are encouraged to pursue the in-depth resources listed at the end of this chapter to develop more knowledge and skills in this area.

What Makes It Comprehensive?

The school counselor's office is often depicted as the place students go (a) if they have a problem, (b) if they're going to college, or (c) if they need their schedules changed. However, a program that is comprehensive is for *all* students—those in school-to-work programs, gifted and talented individuals, kindergarten students beginning their school careers, students with disabilities and academic challenges, the acting-out child, the star athlete, and the shy individual with hidden talents. *All* students need to have regular access to information, activities, resources, and services as a part of their school experience.

Many statewide models of comprehensive developmental guidance and counseling programs are patterned after the "Missouri Model" developed by Norm Gysbers and associates at the University of Missouri. Briefly stated, the model organizes the program into four major components: guidance curriculum, individual planning, responsive services, and system support (sometimes referred to as program management). Too many school counseling programs spend inordinate amounts of time in the responsive services arena, providing individual and small-group counseling and consultation. There are enough problems that need attention in schools so that counselors could always have more than enough to do just focusing on "putting out fires." However, this is seen as a reactive mode of operation, not a proactive model. A developmental model, on the other hand, tries to minimize reactive services and put most of its energy into preventive efforts. *Lessons for Life* puts its emphasis on the other three areas of the Missouri Model. The combined volumes of *Lessons for Life* provide a systemic model for a comprehensive program. The lesson plans offer a comprehensive guidance curriculum that delivers the content students will need to facilitate their individual planning.

For such a program to be comprehensive, it needs to be *thorough* in addressing a range of topics that meets the needs of all youth in the school. The range of topics needs to reflect students' developmental needs, the community's priorities, and significant state or national initiatives. However, this thoroughness can only be provided with respect to the time, personnel, and resources of each unique setting. Therefore, a systematic way of determining topical priorities should be employed. Essentially, a topical map will help the school "cover the territory," so all the travelers' needs can receive attention and all the major landmarks are seen in perspective.

Last but not least, a comprehensive program needs to include more than just school counselors in the delivery of the program. Teachers, specialists, administrators, parents, community members, and students can all play critical roles in adding depth and substance to the activities and services that make up the program. While the counselors—and preferably an advisory committee—will remain responsible for *managing* how all these people are used, the program will be enriched by involving the whole school and the whole community.

Why Should It Be Developmental?

The guidance and counseling program is the gatekeeper of students' social, educational, and career development while they are in school. Developmental psychology recognizes that there are important challenges, processes, and opportunities that students must address as they experience the various stages of their evolving selves. A quality guidance and counseling program anticipates the basic developmental transitions that students will face and attempts to facilitate those transitions in didactic, nurturing, and supportive ways.

Such a program also recognizes that some students will face greater challenges than others or have circumstances in their lives that serve to thwart their development. For these students, developmental *counseling* is needed to help put them back on track as quickly as possible and to avoid further complications. This is where the responsive services component of the total program is seen in perspective.

To efficiently serve the developmental needs of *all* students, a guidance curriculum needs to be created that identifies the developmental topics or issues that are critical for student development and the most appropriate grade levels at which the topics should be addressed. According to Robert Myrick, a noted authority on developmental guidance and counseling programs, "developmental guidance and counseling assumes that human nature moves individuals sequentially and positively toward self-enhancement."

In the "life as a journey" metaphor used in this book, the developmental aspect of the program tries to determine the itinerary and the major "stops" along the way. Developmentalists need to be attuned to when "rest stops" may be needed, as well.

What's the Difference between Guidance and Counseling?

Those of you trying to understand this model for the first time may be wondering why both the terms guidance and counseling are used in describing the program. The term *guidance* has been called vague, confusing, and archaic by some authors in the field. However, others (including the authors of this book) prefer to retain the term, since including such activities or services as career fairs, group test interpretations, public relations initiatives, and computer searches under *school counseling* is both confusing and misleading. For the purposes of assisting educators with the *Lessons for Life* curriculum, the following definitions will be used:

Counseling: Counseling relationships are defined as ongoing helping processes, confidential in nature, that assist people in focusing on personal concerns, planning strategies to address specific issues, and evaluating their success in carrying out these plans. Successful counseling relationships require a high level of knowledge about human development and behavior, as well as effective and facilitative communication skills.

Developmental Guidance: School-wide activities and services are designed to help students focus on the attainment of knowledge and skills for developing healthy life goals and acquiring the behaviors to reach those goals. In elementary, middle, and high schools, these developmental services are aimed at helping students focus on tasks and issues appropriate for their age and stage of life.

How Is It a Program?

Too many school counselors have a conglomeration of services and activities without having a program. Such situations usually result in the counselors' being misunderstood and unappreciated. Program management skills are necessary to properly initiate, integrate, articulate, implement, and be accountable for a well-rounded and well-run program. There needs to be a systemic unity to all the components of the program. Unless all the key players are in agreement on the conceptual framework of the program and are able to adequately explain the program to students, colleagues, superiors, and the public, very little support will be generated to nurture the program's development. This is an area where counselors need to have a perspective on the lay of the land for their own programs and their own school districts, so they can more effectively tell others where they are coming from, where they are now, and where they are going.

Educators using the *Lessons for Life* materials should examine the resources in light of the existing program in the school. If it is not understood how lessons will complement the school's mission and the guidance and counseling program's goals, then time should be devoted to engaging people in a discussion about these important issues. If no leadership is being provided in the area of guidance program management, then action steps should be taken to assure that someone in a leadership position takes coursework or in-service training, reads current literature, or receives consultation assistance to gain these important skills.

THE GUIDANCE CURRICULUM

While all aspects of a comprehensive developmental school guidance and counseling program are important, the guidance curriculum is at the very heart of the program. Without it, counselors are merely seen as providing a conglomeration of services. The guidance curriculum is the vehicle for *delivering* a program that is truly comprehensive and developmental. The guidance curriculum is also seen as an integral part of the total school's curriculum, not as an add-on. As much as possible, the guidance curriculum should be integrated with subject area curricula so that students can see the interrelationships in their learning and the practical applications of the guidance lessons.

If, in assessing the lay of the land in your district, you discover that there is no guidance curriculum, then *Lessons for Life* can help you decide what is needed in your school to address students' developmental needs in the areas of self-knowledge, life roles, educational development, and career exploration and planning. However, if your school does have a guidance curriculum, the task at hand is to review that curriculum to see if "the whole territory" is being covered or whether there are some blank spots on the map. If you're lucky, you may find that your school is doing everything it should be doing. In such a case, put on the cruise control and enjoy the scenery!

Just as "seeing the big picture" is important in the total management of the guidance and counseling program, this same kind of broad visioning is also valued in curriculum development. According to Allan Glatthorn, writing in a publication of the Association for Supervision and Curriculum Development, there are four major considerations in gaining a good grasp of the big picture:

(a) *Knowing what elements will shape your work.* Keep in mind national, state, and local guidelines and initiatives. The National Career Development Guidelines and the SCANS Report, mentioned later in this chapter, are examples of the kinds of elements that might shape a larger vision of a comprehensive and substantive curriculum.

(b) *Knowing specifically what you will produce.* A good curriculum should operate according to a mutually agreed-upon list of goals and topics, a scope-and-sequence framework that targets grade levels and order of presentation, and a list of materials that will assist in the delivery.

(c) *Understanding who will carry out the tasks.* Both the responsibilities for overseeing the total curriculum and the identification of individuals who will actually deliver its lessons require careful thought and attention. Both management and implementation factors are at work here, but the key question should be "Who can be most effective in helping students learn these important lessons?" It may be that a teacher, a parent, a community member, a school custodian, or a peer helper might be the most resourceful or persuasive individual for facilitating particular lessons. However, all particpants need to be aware of their responsibilities and they must be able to plan accordingly, so managing assignments is a crucial need.

(d) *Identifying what needs to be done to carry out the tasks.* Staff development, selection of textbooks (or integrated curriculum handbooks), and decisions about authentic assessment of the curriculum and student competencies are critical aspects of being accountable for a quality curriculum. Decisions in these areas should be made in the context of existing plans and procedures within a school system. Educators using *Lessons for Life* should also view these three areas of accountability as critical factors for successfully transitioning to a new and more fully integrated curriculum that is complementary to other programs.

The *Lessons for Life* curriculum materials should be used in the context of this "big picture" framework. Because flexibility has been built into the lessons, educators can adapt and adopt lessons according to local needs or national guidelines, according to the scope and sequence plan of an individual teacher or an entire district, and according to the unique talents or preferences of those who will be delivering the lessons. However, everyone should be operating from the same basic map.

NATIONAL MODELS OF EXCELLENCE

Some schools like to use national models of excellence to establish the "content validity" of their work. (Remember that concept from your research class?) Since two such models were used by the American School Counselor Association in the development of the *Get a Life* portfolio, and because they are in keeping with the comprehensive developmental model that was just explained, they are offered here as examples of how theoretical frameworks can provide more credibility for a program's efforts. The National Career Development Guidelines and the SCANS Competencies are holistic models that have been well received by the lay public and legislative bodies alike.

National Career Development Guidelines

During the 1980s, a cadre of national leaders in various career development groups joined forces to create the National Career Development (NCD) Guidelines (National Occupational Information Coordinating Committee, 1988), identifying the competencies needed to be successful in a global economy and society. The Guidelines are seen as a *complement* to a comprehensive developmental program, rather than as a conflicting model. Essentially, the Guidelines provide a well-grounded framework for a comprehensive program, and they are especially appealing to administrators, school board members, and parents because they provide a practical, commonsense, and understandable approach to empowering youth. The *Get a Life* portfolio was created to demonstrate the compatibility of the comprehensive developmental school counseling and guidance program model and the National Career Development Guidelines, and to provide a tangible resource for schools to use in assisting youth with the development of their career competencies.

As a national model, the National Career Development Guidelines offer schools a "way of the land." At least eight national associations have endorsed the NCD Guidelines, recommending that they be used for creating high-quality programs. The guidelines provide hierarchically arranged competencies at the elementary school, middle school, high school, and adult levels, illustrating that career development is a lifelong venture. As stated in the introduction to the Guidelines, "they provide a blueprint of career development competencies that children, youth, and adults should master, and identify standards or indicators of evidence that individuals have attained those competencies."

Schools do not have to accept the National Career Development Guidelines as the only acceptable model, but counselors, students, parents, and the community should commit themselves to some model of career development. The message to students needs to be clear: Career development is not just about "getting jobs"; it's about "getting a life!" A holistic, balanced perspective on life (one's ultimate career) development is what every school should be aspiring to promote as one of its major goals.

Most career development models advocate a three-dimensional paradigm for emphasizing Self-Knowledge, Educational Development, and Occupational Exploration and Planning as interconnected components of the broader concept of one's career. The *Get a Life* portfolio model used some editorial license to incorporate several important topics from those three components into a fourth area called "Life Roles," thus emphasizing the critical importance of such factors as family aspirations, cultural heritage, sex-role stereotyping, and peer influences in nurturing or limiting one's career development. These three (or four) categories can provide an organizational and conceptual framework for a school's guidance curriculum. It becomes obvious in this book that this four-part framework was the organizational scheme for the *Lessons for Life* curriculum.

The SCANS Report

During the early 1990s, the Secretary's Commission on Achieving Necessary Skills (SCANS) was directed to advise the U.S. Secretary of Labor on the level of skills required for young people to meet the demands of a global economy and a workforce that was increasingly dependent on technology. The commission explored the current situation and future needs in American schools and the American workplace through extensive discussions, interviews, and meetings with business owners, public employers, unions, and workers and supervisors in shops, plants, and stores. The prevailing message from their research was:

> Good jobs will increasingly depend on people who can put knowledge to work. What we found was disturbing: more than half our young people leave school without the knowledge or foundation required to find and hold a good job. These young people will pay a very high price. They face the bleak prospects of dead-end work interrupted only by periods of unemployment. (SCANS, 1992, p. xv)

The message was not intended so much as a portent of doom but as a call to action. This was a "wake-up call" to schools and communities and governments to take responsible steps to reform educational systems so that students could be prepared for the demands of the twenty-first century. As one becomes familiar with the lay of the land, it becomes obvious that the "way" of the land is to become more aware of the "way of the world." The SCANS Report became a significant document in influencing future legislation and national and state initiatives to make education more relevant to students' and communities' and the nation's needs. You will find the language of the SCANS Report infused in many of the school reform documents generated by state legislatures and departments of education during the past few years, as well as federal legislation like the School-to-Work Opportunities Act of 1994.

A major recommendation of the SCANS Report was that schools find ways to promote "workplace know-how" which would lead to effective job performance. This know-how has two elements: competencies and a foundation. The report advocated that five major competencies and a three-part foundation of skills and personal qualities be "taught and understood in an integrated fashion that reflects the workplace *contexts* in which they are applied" (p. xv). In other words, the commission recommended that learning take place within the real environment, as much as possible, instead of operating within an abstract framework that students could not fully appreciate.

The five major SCANS competencies are in the areas of Resources (identifies, organizes, plans, and allocates resources); Interpersonal (works with others); Information (acquires and uses information); Systems (understands complex interrelationships); and Technology (works with a variety of technologies). Careful examination will reveal that many of the competencies are already a part of most schools' curricula. For example, under the Information section students should be able to "interpret and communicate information"—certainly an integral aspect of most language arts programs. Other competencies are very commonsense, practical items that probably *should* be part of every curriculum, but perhaps are not. Under the Interpersonal section, for example, the SCANS competencies suggest that all students should be able to "negotiate—work toward agreements involving exchange of resources; resolve[s] divergent interests." Still other competencies reflect the technological, global diversity, and economic realities of our changing world and must be infused in curricula to help students succeed in life.

The three-part foundation explained in the SCANS document addresses **Basic Skills** (reading, writing, listening, mathematics, and speaking), **Thinking Skills** (creative thinking, problem solving, decision making, knowing how to learn, seeing with the mind's eye, and reasoning), and **Personal Qualities** (responsibility, self-esteem, sociability, self-management, and integrity/honesty). While the first area (Basic Skills) is often the focus of the school's curriculum, the SCANS Report emphasized that the thinking skills and personal qualities also needed increased attention if students were to be prepared to work in a high-performance workplace.

The *Get a Life* portfolio includes many items from the SCANS competencies and three-part foundation, demonstrating that these important aspects of Self-Knowledge are an integral part of one's career development. As a result, *Lessons for Life* includes several lesson plans for helping students explore their own competence in these areas.

REFLECTIVE LEARNERS/PRODUCTIVE EARNERS

Authentic assessment is one of the current buzzwords in the educational reform movement. Authentic assessment goes beyond performance assessment in that students not only complete or demonstrate a desired behavior, but they do so in the context of real-life applications. There are several complex facets of authenticity—such as task complexity, motivation, locus of control, and criteria standards—that might be considered which suggest that it is a higher order of applied assessment and that it requires careful deliberation and execution if it is to be used effectively with students.

Portfolios are examples of authentic assessment that recognize that norm-referenced tests and imposed standards are insufficient measures for the very significant personal learning that is required for students to truly value the learning process. Portfolios tap into an "internal accountability" process that encourages students, teachers, families, and even community members to think hard about the essential learning that helps individuals to make sense of their world (get the lay of the land) and to think about what evidence can be provided to demonstrate progress and success.

It is easy to see why portfolios are becoming increasingly popular in today's schools. Educators can certainly use the *Lessons for Life* curriculum materials independently of the portfolio model; however, portfolios should be considered as a viable option in providing learning experiences that are more comprehensive and attentive to developmental growth, personal discovery, and empowerment. Part of those learning experiences must include assessment that is more authentic and significant for "personal meaning-making."

Essentially, the portfolio becomes a tool to help students reflect upon learning experiences according to their own life experiences and perspectives. If they are encouraged to put their best thinking and best work into the portfolio, it becomes a conduit and receptacle for the significant pieces of work that define their standards and levels of meaning. As reflective learners, they begin to appreciate the need to refine their thinking, their writing, and their contributions to the portfolio.

Since the lesson plans in *Lessons for Life* were created to accompany a nationally validated career (life) development portfolio model, students should have many insights and questions and decisions to reflect upon as they examine who they are and what they want for themselves. By developmentally sequencing lessons in the areas of Self-Knowledge, Life Roles, Educational Development, and Career Exploration and Planning, schools can be instrumental in shaping the "internal accountability" that will assist youth in some of the most significant decision making of their lives. Certainly, one of our goals is to produce *productive earners* in a global economy; however, we also want to produce *reflective learners* who know how to attach their own standards of meaning to the significant questions they will face in life. The lessons in this book applied to a portfolio model can provide a wonderful vehicle for empowering youth to become both reflective learners and productive earners—and in the process, offer a model for learning that can last a lifetime. As travelers on life's journey, they will have more security in moving from one destination to the next because they will have the "lay of the land."

SUMMARY

In this chapter, we have tried to summarize some of the foundational or conceptual underpinnings of the *Lessons for Life* curriculum materials. An appreciation for the evolving significance of these models and guidelines can lend perspective to the rationale behind the lessons in this book and, more important, to the roles you can play in helping youth set an agenda for career/life planning that is personally meaningful and rewarding.

"Seeing the big picture" is only part of the process. Effective educators use such a broad conceptual framework to create their own meaning-making, so they can, in turn, interpret the big picture in enlightening and facilitative ways so that the students benefit from their vision. Those who truly see the big picture also recognize that as educators we must be role models, examples of reflective learners in the midst of our own "process." Therefore, it is hoped that some of this information will trigger questions and further investigation in the areas of career guidance program management, career development, guidance curriculum planning, and authentic assessment. As tour guides for the trip of a lifetime, your own adventures should provide you with more than enough insights about what the landscape really looks like.

REFERENCES

Baker, S. B. *School Counseling for the Twenty-first Century.* New York: Merrill, 1992.

Glatthorn, A. A. *Developing a Quality Curriculum.* Alexandria, VA: ASCD, 1994.

Gysbers, N. C. & Henderson, P. *Developing and Managing Your School Guidance Program.* Alexandria, VA: ACA, 1988.

Meyer, C. A. "What's the difference between authentic and performance assessment?" *Educational Leadership,* May 1992: 39-40.

Myrick, R. D. *Developmental Guidance and Counseling: A Practical Approach* (2nd edition). Minneapolis: Educational Media, 1993.

NOICC. *National Career Development Guidelines.* Washington, DC: National Occupational Information Coordinating Committee (NOICC), 1989; 1996.

Schmidt, J. J. *Counseling in Schools: Essential Services and Comprehensive Programs.* Boston: Allyn & Bacon, 1992.

School-to-Work Opportunities Act of 1994, 20 U.S.C.A. § 6111 *et seq.*

Secretary's Commission on Achieving Necessary Skills. *What Work Requires of Schools: A SCANS Report for America 2000.* Washington, DC: U.S. Department of Labor, 1991.

VanZandt, C. E. & Hayslip, J. B. *Your Comprehensive School Guidance and Counseling Program: A Handbook of Practical Activities.* New York: Longman, 1994.

VanZandt, C. E., Perry, N. S., & Brawley, K. T. *Get a Life: Your Personal Planning Portfolio for Career Development.* Alexandria, VA: ASCA, 1993.

Wolf, D. P., LeMahieu, P. G., & Eresh, J. "Good measure: Assessment as a tool for educational reform." *Educational Leadership,* May 1992: 8-13.

CHAPTER THREE

Planning the Trip

Practical Tips for Settings Things in Motion

Because the lessons in this book represent a departure from the more traditional delivery systems and focus more on a preventive and integrated approach to empowering youth, we want to share a few suggestions and considerations that may assist you in organizing and delivering the lessons. These practical issues are mostly common sense, but are worth repeating because of their significance in fostering the success of your program. Even though you may have taken this trip before, it is always a good idea to check your plans to make sure you have not forgotten anything.

In the deliberations about how things get done, the students and their needs are central to all our planning. This chapter on management issues starts with the larger mission in mind, then proceeds to the more specific needs of instructors and individual students. This systemic perspective highlights the importance of everyone following the same map so that people don't get lost along the way.

The first section focuses on management issues that relate to both school politics and program delivery. The second section attends to classroom issues and provides information, techniques, and suggestions for enhancing the learning experiences of students as they participate in the *Lessons for Life* curriculum. Finally, we offer a few notes about student concerns that may surface as they participate in cooperative learning experiences and become more adept at being reflective learners.

These practical suggestions are offered in a snapshot format so that you can quickly scan the entire chapter to get a sense of the variety of concerns that need to be considered in planning and delivering a quality career guidance curriculum. You are encouraged to pursue more in-depth reading on topics that are of particular concern to you.

MANAGEMENT ISSUES

Administrative Support

Know the people who can act on your behalf when questions are asked and decisions are made about program priorities, resource allocations, and budget requests. Successful programs recognize the importance of administrative support and involvement. In business, employees wouldn't (or shouldn't, anyway) plan trips without management recognizing how the trips support the company's mission. The trips often carry more significance, as well, if the CEO goes along on the junket. The same thinking holds true in schools.

Involve the Principal. Your key ally in promoting curricular change in a building is the school's administrator. Educate your principal about *Lessons for Life*. Show how this curriculum complements the school's curriculum. Reinforce how attention to students' developmental needs can promote better learning. Keep your principal informed so he or she can address faculty and community concerns as knowledgeably as the counselor or the coordinator of the *Lessons for Life* curriculum. (Principals hate to be caught off-guard. Can you blame them?)

Keep District Administrators Informed. If you have a Curriculum Coordinator, work closely with that person to build support for the career guidance curriculum and to make sure *Lessons for Life* materials are aligned with district guidelines. If your district does not have a Curriculum Coordinator, be sure to work with your principal to apprise the superintendent of any curricular changes you make.

Appreciate the Power of School Boards. Recognize that with all the decisions school board members have to make (as volunteers), they need concise, informative communication to help them understand why your program is important. At least twice a year, update them on the success of your program.

Create an Advisory Committee. Choose active members of the school and community who can offer ideas, feedback, and perspective, while also sharing their enthusiasm for the curriculum and/or the guidance and counseling program, if that is where *Lessons for Life* will be the focus. Meet three or four times a year. Strike a balance between asking them to do too much and having them "rubber stamp" everything you tell them you are doing. Advisory committee members can be some of the best spokespersons for your program.

Public Relations

Most people only see small snippets of your curriculum or program and draw conclusions about its worth and effectiveness based on that inadequate information. You must find a way to creatively, concisely, coherently, and correctly portray both your goals and your accomplishments. The school year only allows time for about three or four major PR projects, so choose the ones that will maximize your message!

Use Informational Letters to Parents. An introductory letter that explains the new *Lessons for Life* curriculum should include the benefits and purposes, as well as examples of some of the lessons. If your school is using the *Get a Life* portfolio, this would also be a good time to introduce it. Later, letters like the one accompanying the "What's in a Name?" lesson (in the Life Roles section) may be sent home to encourage parent involvement in learning activities.

Promote Community Networking. There are a variety of ways to involve the community. Some of the lessons encourage students to talk with community members. Set the stage for such involvement by meeting with groups like the Chamber of Commerce or local service clubs to discuss community-based learning opportunities. Agree to speak at luncheons or meetings where you can give an overview of the curriculum, show examples of how students are involved in their career development, and seek volunteers who would like to contribute their time or resources.

Press for Media Coverage. Use local cable or network television and radio stations, as well as newspapers, to illustrate the highlights of your program. Share some good news for a change. Invite students and community members to be a part of the press coverage.

Offer Interesting Events. Use National School Counseling Week, a Career Fair, the National Career Development Month Poster Contest, Aspirations Day, or some other event to showcase some of the special features of your program or curriculum. Invite or include parents and the public.

Logistical Planning

Just as a long family automobile trip is usually more successful if you have an itinerary, a good roadmap, a well-tuned and comfortable car, good drivers, and a cooperative family, a successful curriculum requires similar features. Attention to critical logistical matters can help make the transition to a new curriculum run a lot more smoothly.

Create a Scope-and-Sequence Chart.   Visually outline the grade and time of year that various topics or lessons will be offered. This will help school board members, administrators, teachers, and parents see "the big picture" more clearly. It will also help those who are implementing the curriculum be better organized and focused. If all topics or lessons are not going to be used, this is the time to decide which ones will be omitted (and why).

Conduct In-Service Training.   Adjusting to a new curriculum is a developmental process. In the early stages, teachers (and any others who will be implementing the curriculum) will need a broad overview of the total curriculum and where the changes are taking place, a rationale for why the change is important, information about resources, expectations, and responsibilities, and as much as possible, practical activities that familiarize them with the lessons and materials. Conduct in-service training for administrators, as well, to keep them up to date and knowledgeable. Last but not least, properly train volunteers so that they understand the school's expectations and the parameters of their responsibilities, and make sure they have the resources, knowledge, and skills to do a good job.

Develop a Schedule.   Anybody and everybody who is involved in this curriculum needs to know who does what and when! Share the responsibility, but coordinate the lessons so that conflicts are avoided and learning opportunities are optimized.

Plan Ahead.   Develop a master list of supplies, library resources, room assignments, community contacts, guest speakers, A-V equipment, etc., that will be needed by those implementing the curriculum. If individuals are given the responsibility for addressing these considerations on their own, create a grid sheet that all can use to organize their planning in a similar fashion. The librarians, technicians, guest speakers, etc., will appreciate uniform practices. If supplies or materials need to be included in the annual budget, this advanced planning can help delineate program needs and priorities.

Accountability

Parents, administrators, faculty, school board members, students, and interested community members are either curious or concerned about whether change has been worth it. The quality of accountability information is much more important than quantity.

Collect Evaluation Information.   Both quantitative and qualitative evaluations can assess the effectiveness or support for your program or curriculum. Determine what you think your accountability audiences would like to know (ask them), then create methods for gathering the information. Use local colleges and universities as resources if this seems a formidable task.

Conduct a Needs Assessment.   You could use the advisory committee or a sample of students, teachers, or parents to determine whether the curriculum needs to address other topics that are not currently covered. Compare this information with the evaluation data.

Carry Out Research.   Again, involve your local college professors or research centers to help with this need if research is not your forte. Remember that good research data can be a powerful tool for demonstrating both needs and results.

Involve Advisory Committee in Program Review.   One of the greatest ways an advisory committee can assist a program is to seek information and clarify issues that reflect the year's progress in meeting program goals. Advisory committee members can (a) analyze evaluation and needs assessment data, (b) integrate needs assessment information with other input and materials presented to them, and (c) offer their concerns, commendations, and recommendations for fostering better programming and meeting more needs.

Submit an Annual Report.   As concisely as possible, summarize the year, give examples of successes and problems, list concise evaluative data, make conclusions and recommendations—and as much as possible, *blow your own horn*!

Storage and Retrieval

One of the "most-asked" questions about portfolios is where they should be stored. There is no single best place to keep such materials because every school's situation is unique. Much depends on the space and resources available in individual schools. The materials needed for the *Lessons for Life* curriculum present similar challenges. The important thing for your school is that you recognize the need to address the problem, brainstorm some possible solutions, decide on the best plan in terms of its efficiency and accommodation of needs, then put the plan into practice.

CLASSROOM ISSUES

Readiness

The foundation for presenting anything new to people is to create a level of readiness that makes them feel secure in that change. If students see *Lessons for Life* (or the *Get a Life* portfolio if you are using it) as something new and exciting, they will anticipate the change with wonder. Planning a trip shouldn't be a drudgery. It should help the travelers look forward to the journey with high expectations.

Create a "Build-Up" That Gets Students Excited.   Start early (even during the previous spring) and use bulletin boards, school newsletters, PA announcements, T-shirts, displays, etc. to give "sound bytes" that tantalize students about the upcoming curriculum (e.g., Got a Life? Get One Next Fall! ... or ... Life-Altering Changes Next Fall!). Lay the foundation for this curriculum being something special ... and fun.

Help Students See the "Big Picture."   As you explain the *Lessons for Life* curriculum to students, demonstrate its relevance to their lives, the needs of the local community, the economic outlook of your state, national agendas, and the global economy. Also, link the curriculum to their K-12 educational process and to your school's integrated curriculum (if you have one, of course).

Emphasize That Career Is a PROCESS, Not an Event.   "What do you want to be when you grow up?" is one of those (inappropriate) questions that assumes there is one perfect job to which individuals should aspire and they should figure out what it is when they're young. The reality is that people usually make several major career changes in their lives, so learning a *process* of making career decisions is much more important than finalizing one's choice. One's career is also a process of integrating a job "career" with family, social, leisure, spiritual, and community "careers." Since one's career is a complex process of human development, it should not be viewed as a simplistic decision.

Explain *Lessons for Life* As a Total Package.   Let students explore the meaning of the package of lessons they are being offered as a part of the career guidance curriculum. Although the lessons are designed so they can be used independently of or as a complement to the *Get a Life* portfolio, explaining how the lessons fit together as a group of activities that will help students make more sense out of their lives is an important message.

Teaching and Learning

Learning can certainly take place in the absence of teaching, but learning is enhanced by good teaching. Therefore, we'd like to share some lessons of teaching that may assist those who may be new to the process of facilitating student learning.

Model Instructor/Facilitator Enthusiasm for the Lessons.   So much of what we communicate is nonverbal; therefore, we need to project messages to students that say, "This lesson is important." By sharing personal anecdotes that relate to the lessons, teachers are able to demonstrate how personal decision making was (or could have been) a critical aspect of their own development. In the process, students understand the lessons' relevancy.

Reinforce Rules of Group Behavior.   Come to a consensus of group rules (e.g., No put-downs, okay to "pass," etc.) and post them on the chalkboard or bulletin board. Refer to the rules as guidelines for both classroom and small-group behavior.

Be Sure That Lessons Are Understood and Supplies Are in Place.   A very good lesson can come unravelled if poor directions or missing materials keep students from having "all the parts of the puzzle." A five-minute readiness check can help focus the lesson.

Share the Lesson Objectives.   Don't keep the objectives of your lessons a secret. It's okay to let students guess what they think the objectives were after the lesson (a quick evaluation device) as long as they aren't kept in the dark about the abilities they should be able to demonstrate as the result of a lesson.

Don't Bite Off More Than Kids Can Chew.   In our experiences with teachers using the *Get a Life* portfolio for the first time, we've seen many try to have their students fill in an entire *page* of the portfolio in one 45-minute class! Sometimes 45 minutes won't be enough time to fill in a single *frame* on the page because the topic or issue is too complex for students to comprehend, ponder, write about, share, reflect upon, revise, commit to, and rewrite. A combination of professional expertise and common sense will help you determine whether students are developmentally ready to handle the complexities of a lesson. A significant value of portfolio work is the gift of time it gives students to reflect upon the experiences, and to process the information prior to making a final entry.

Make Directions Understandable.   New teachers usually need to read directions verbatim when introducing an exercise to make sure they don't miss anything. Nothing wrong with that! With lesson familiarity, you may develop a more natural delivery and be able to explain the directions instead of reading them. Whatever your comfort level, the important thing to keep in mind is that students must clearly understand what it is they are to do.

Be Flexible.   We mentioned flexibility as one of the trademarks of *Lessons for Life*. Try the lessons once and then decide whether or not you want to add your own flair to an exercise, or adapt it in a particular way that will more effectively meet students' needs or more appropriately reflect your style of teaching. We encourage you to make notes on the lesson plans for future reference.

Reinforce Earlier Lessons.   It may be necessary to remind students of lessons they had previously that can serve as a foundation for a current lesson. Don't assume that all students will see the connections among lessons. Lessons that were particularly fun and/or successful can be especially powerful in getting across fundamental concepts that can enhance a new lesson.

Nurture the Art of Questioning.   In reflective learning, students are encouraged to ponder questions that help them sort out their own levels of meaning and insight. Genuine questioning is at the core of learning, so students need to feel that their questions are valued—both by the instructors and their peers. An atmosphere of acceptance needs to be fostered so that all students feel comfortable asking either basic or profound questions whose answers lead to greater understanding.

Create a Sense of Closure to Lessons.   A few structured moments spent at the end of each lesson will be helpful for most students to put the learning in perspective. The closure questions in *Lessons for Life* allow you to develop this focus. If time runs out at the end of a lesson, be sure to review the lesson in the next session with the class to make sure they have really captured the basic objectives of the lesson. Closure is also helpful in getting students ready to make the transition to more didactic (and less personal) lessons in their next class.

Build in Time for Reflection and Making Entries in the Portfolios.   If portfolio entries are supposed to represent the students' best thinking and best work, then sufficient time must be devoted to the process of reflection and refining one's work. While some of this reflection and refinement may be done outside class, teachers should try to occasionally observe the process in class, as well. As both an informal assessment and a reality check, teachers can learn much from the way students address the reflective learning process.

Recognize the "Teachable Moments." Because students bring their unique lives to the learning process, it is imperative that we tune in to the topics, activities, discussions, and questions that capture their fascination, cause wonderment, or motivate them in some way to learn or explore for their own sakes. The signs are sometimes subtle (a furrowed eyebrow or leaning forward in a chair) or they might be as obvious as the hands-in-the-air "Ah-hah" gestures or an excited smile, but a good teacher recognizes the need to foster the teachable moment with genuine interest and reinforcement, and sees the possibility of new learning being attached to this moment. There will also be times when it becomes obvious that an entire class is captivated in a teachable moment and the teacher seizes the moment and runs with it—and prays that there will be many more days like this!

Learn from Minor Disasters. There may be times when the very best of lessons "backfire." In such situations, the lesson needs to be analyzed from different points of view. The content, dynamics of the class, the delivery, other events taking place in school, environmental factors, or the basic "chemistry" of the classroom should all be considered in trying to determine why things did not work this time.

Cooperative Learning Foundation

Cooperative learning is the preferred model for *Lessons for Life*. Much can be gained from the interactions of youth as they share their insights, aspirations, questions, and needs. Although the lessons can be adapted to fit the instructor's style, we offer the following highlights of cooperative learning for those who may be unfamiliar with the technique and want to try it out.

Teach Group Process Techniques As the Framework for Cooperative Learning. Whole courses are taught on group process skills, but the following are the basics to which school students should attend:

- *Team-building*—Create activities that allow group members to appreciate individual strengths and needs in the small groups. Foster collaboration versus competition. Plan team-building activities that fit the developmental needs of students. A frivolous hand-holding exercise may be fine for younger students, but the older ones may find it too "touchy-feely" and immature. Two or three team-building activities may be needed before group members begin to recognize each other's strengths and contributions to the team's work.

- *Stages of groups*—Common names for the developmental stages of groups are Forming, Storming, Norming, and Performing (and eventually Adjourning). In the second stage, appreciating that the group *should* experience some frustration, confusion, and disorientation as ideas and questions are shared and goals are defined is reassuring to both students and facilitators. The key to moving successfully through the storming stage is using good communication skills. The most important communication skill is listening. Task-oriented individuals often struggle with this stage because they become impatient with the group spending so much time on understanding each other. The instructor needs to encourage and model patience with the process as the group eventually moves to wonderful levels of creativity and productivity *if* they stay focused and they make sure all group members are included and valued.

- *Leadership in groups*—Every group should have a leader who is assigned or elected. Shared leadership rarely works. Having a designated leader gives one person some permission to move the group toward its goal without seeming too pushy. The group may even want to talk about the kind of leader or leadership they want to help them be successful.

- *Roles students play*—Every group member plays one or more roles in the group. Without leadership or direction, some of the unwanted roles might be joker, shirker, loafer, devil's advocate, troublemaker, pain-in-the-neck … you get the idea! The "Understanding Roles" lessons in the Life Roles section of *Lessons for Life* focus on the positive roles students can play in group situations. It is often helpful in cooperative learning groups to have members discuss the various roles that will be necessary for their group to be successful, then have members assume responsibility for playing those necessary roles as the group works together.

- *Norms*—Get the groups to list a few basic rules or guidelines that will help them work well together and accomplish their tasks. For example, "no name calling," "respect others' ideas," and "do your best work" are the kinds of norms that often surface. By posting the norms near where the group works, the leaders or instructors can refer to the list when a group starts to wander from its norms. A basic, manageable list is better than a lengthy one.

Establish an Environment of Trust.   Beyond the basics of group process skills, students also need to trust that the cooperative learning process will work and that they can trust their classmates to be considerate of their needs and individuality. Simple looks or statements can destroy trust. Some of the "Interpersonal Skills" lessons in the Self-Knowledge section discuss the importance of good communication skills, which are key factors in building trust.

Specify and Clarify Group Tasks.   What seems clear to some will appear confusing to others. It's just the nature of things. If lessons call for specific tasks to be accomplished, make sure students fully understand what is expected. Promote questioning as an important part of communicating and understanding. If everyone in the group operates according to the same understanding, then more cohesiveness and cooperation will follow.

Process the Process.   At the very heart of the cooperative learning model is the notion that students need time to reflect on their learning. The process of self-discovery, the process of career decision making, the process of learning in groups, the process of analyzing the depth and meaning of a lesson—all require time and a process for "personal meaning-making." Two of the more obvious ways to accomplish this "processing" are through individual reflection (such as making entries in a journal, a portfolio, or on a worksheet) and group discussion. By sharing and asking questions in groups, students broaden their perspective on issues, learn a more expansive vocabulary to apply to their life development, and benefit from a kind of "spectator therapy," whereby they learn from the insights and discoveries of others. A strong foundation of group process skills makes "processing the process" a natural extension of the *Lessons for Life* exercises.

Classroom Discipline

The primary ingredient of strong classroom discipline is an exciting curriculum that makes learning fun, relevant, and attainable. We also recognize that the strongest curriculum and the most gifted instructors will still encounter discipline problems on occasion. Our advice is to (a) remain respectful to all; (b) refer to agreed-upon and posted rules; (c) model problem-solving or conflict-resolution skills, if applicable; (d) place reasonable limits on behavior and state your expectations for acceptable behavior; and (e) ask that any student who cannot comply with those limits be removed until willing to comply with expected norms.

When a lesson appears to be going "downhill," we encourage teachers to set the plans aside and analyze the situation with the class. Simply asking "What seems to be happening here?" may lead to an answer or an awareness that allows the lesson to continue—or to be postponed to address a more timely issue.

Homework Assignments

Several of the lessons in this book include homework assignments that complement or serve as extensions of those lessons. Homework doesn't have to be (and shouldn't be) a drudgery. The following are key aspects of using homework with *Lessons for Life*.

Involve the Parents. Parents and family members are often the most influential people in students' career decisions. The homework assignments are designed to let family members and significant adults share important lessons they have learned about the world of work, what's important in life, and what mistakes to avoid. There are also opportunities to share cultural and ethnic customs and unique perspectives which are so much a part of an individual's development.

See the Community As a Classroom. Students need a view of the real world, and the local community provides concrete realities, and practical opportunities, as well as abstract possibilities about the world of career development. Homework assignments that encourage youth to learn from their communities also promote a better understanding of the communities as a result of their investigations.

Timing and Workload. If homework assignments from *Lessons for Life* are tacked on to students' workloads when they already have a long list of papers, exams, and projects for which they must study, they may see the assignments as just one more burden of being a student. Allowing ample time for assignments and being attentive to other important class projects, athletic events, vacations, and extracurricular activities will help students be more receptive to the lessons and, in turn, model the significance of striking a balance in one's life among the various roles we must play.

When assignments are continually late, it might behoove the teacher or counselor to ask the student to conference privately. Family situations, jobs, and personal problems are often very legitimate excuses for late work. Ask the student to figure out a plan to get the work done. A cooperative spirit often lessens students' personal burdens and gives them more incentive to complete assignments. Again, planning the trip will be more fun and meaningful if the traveler sees the trip as feasible and necessary.

STUDENT ISSUES

Nature of the Beast

Many students may be extremely opinionated about certain topics, due to family background, personal experiences, and peer group culture—or they may just be trying to assert themselves. Adolescents, in particular, are attempting to critically analyze the world about them. Many of the activities in *Lessons for Life* ask for students to investigate and share their personal belief systems. Tolerance of differences may be one of the greatest challenges of this curriculum, as well as one of its greatest accomplishments. It will be important to strike a balance between honoring individual opinions and keeping students from insulting and demeaning others by their opinions. All students need to be encouraged to listen and respect opinions, and respond to opposition with facts rather than personal attacks.

Motivation—Group and Individual

Motivation is foundational to getting students to seriously attend to the career development curriculum. If most members of a classroom are enthusiastic about a lesson, the rest usually will fall in line. Certain individuals within the classroom may also be instrumental in motivating classmates to consider the seriousness of a lesson. Knowing *who* and *what* motivate students will help you focus your energy on *how* to get students invested in their life development in substantive ways.

On an individual basis, what "turns on" one student may "turn off" another. Explaining this fact (and getting students to accept it) often allows students to feel they can share more freely—sometimes even in a negative fashion—and to sort out what motivates them.

Developmental Challenges

Chronological age or grade level never determines a student's developmental maturity. A lesson that seems appropriate for the majority of a class may "miss the mark" with a student who is still struggling with developmental issues that others have already mastered. Patience and understanding must be modeled by adults and nurtured in peers, as students who seem less mature or developmentally ready for some lessons struggle to make sense of their world. Referring back to previous lessons in a section of the book may give hints about topics or issues that a student may need to consider before a current lesson can make sense.

Individual Idiosyncrasies

There will be times when students may resist certain activities, such as role playing, because of self-consciousness or shyness. Describing the format of the activity and encouraging volunteers often eliminates lack of participation. When the whole class balks at an activity, present the objectives and ask them to create an alternative activity that will produce the same results.

Information That Can Be Shared with Others

It should be determined in advance that information shared in a portfolio and in class is not confidential. Students should be encouraged to talk with their teachers and counselors in advance of sharing any personal information that may make others uncomfortable. Should personal insights or issues be shared unexpectedly in class, the lesson facilitator should process the information prior to the end of class. Sometimes all that is needed is a gentle reminder about honoring a person's privacy and dignity. "Teachable moments" such as these can contribute to the developmental and maturational life of students at any age—if handled with respect and sensitivity.

Confidentiality

There may be times when students disclose information in their portfolios or in small group discussions that truly should remain confidential. For example, in the Personal Notes box in the Self-Knowledge section of the *Get a Life* portfolio, occasionally a student might make a statement about suicide or abuse issues. Obviously, such a student is asking for help. The school counselor should be involved and the student should be encouraged to share the concern—but not in the portfolio. If a school does not have a clear policy about confidentiality, then such a policy should become a priority and faculty and staff should be apprised of their responsibilities or obligations.

Special Needs

It is extremely important to take into consideration students' special needs (e.g., auditory processing problems, eye-hand coordination difficulties, writing deficits, etc.). Modification of activities should be made with little disruption to the class and the activity. Students with special needs should be reassured that modifications are considered an essential part of learning.

Individual Planning and Advising

A great deal of personal growth can be attained through group activities; however, some individual contact with a teacher or counselor may be essential for personal, academic, or career planning. Students should be aware of procedures for seeing an advisor for an appointment. Essentially, all the lessons in this book are designed to facilitate individual planning and advising. Individuals need to plan their own lives, but they usually need some advice along the way. It's important to have receptive adults who can appreciate students' individual journeys while lending support when needed.

SUMMARY

Entire college courses are devoted to some of the topics we have discussed in this chapter. We recognize that a single chapter cannot do justice to the importance of the management issues, classroom issues, and student issues that can confound and compound the delivery of a school's curriculum. However, in highlighting some of these important issues, it is our hope that we can both create an appreciation for "the big picture" that complements curriculum implementation and at the same time provide some useful advice that will make the delivery of these lessons more plausible and enjoyable.

A quality developmental career guidance curriculum requires quality management, quality content, and quality instruction. The astute educator will recognize the areas in this chapter that require further study and development, and seek the resources to enhance the knowledge and skills that will assure successful fulfillment of the program goals. Plan the trip accordingly.

And now, let us introduce the *Lessons for Life...*

CHAPTER FOUR

In the Driver's Seat

Lessons to Promote Self-Knowledge

We need to be in the driver's seat when it comes to exploring career options and making important life decisions. Having other people make our career decisions for us is like having a chauffeur—or even worse, a designated driver! If we hand over the wheel to others, we are either admitting that we don't want to be responsible for the ride or we may feel our own driving abilities are impaired. This is one ride on which we can't afford the luxury of letting someone else take the wheel; therefore, we have to assume responsibility and make sure nothing is impairing our ability to enjoy the ride.

When you settle into that driver's seat, only you know what makes you comfortable: Is there enough head room? Is there lumbar support? Can your feet reach the pedals? Does the rearview mirror allow you to see where you've been? Is your seatbelt fastened? Do you have a good grip on the wheel? Is it the kind of vehicle you really enjoy driving? Self-knowledge is the key to feeling confident about and comfortable with the career journey you are about to embark upon. Self-knowledge is critical before any movement of the vehicle is initiated.

Good career choices rely on finding a good "fit" between the individual and the occupation. A comfortable fit in career decision making first of all requires an awareness of what makes the individual unique. Do you prefer working with data, people, things, or ideas? Would you rather work indoors or outdoors? What do you find fascinating? What bores you? What rewards do you seek from work? How important is work related to other things in your life? Recognizing who you are helps give you a clear, "bug-free" windshield. Self-knowledge helps you sit comfortably in the driver's seat and assures you of having a dashboard free of obstacles that could distract you or interfere with your attention to the road. Self-confidence puts you in the driver's seat. Although passengers or back-seat drivers may have opinions or input about which direction you should take or what they think of your driving habits, you are still the one who needs to make the important decisions behind the wheel. Of course, recognizing that those influences can sometimes shift you into forward or reverse is understanding what growth is all about. Being receptive to wise advice may promote changes for the better—and perhaps provide for a smoother and more scenic adventure.

Essentially, self-knowledge provides students with the operator's license to get on the road, and to appreciate the journey. When they begin to define themselves, they can more appropriately interact with peers and adults who can caution and enlighten them about the career process. Self-knowledge is the power that fuels the vehicle of change and growth. Along the journey, total empowerment will rely on regular refueling and maintenance.

This chapter includes lesson plans and activities for helping students find the fuel to start and maintain their career journeys. Five different components of Self-Knowledge are addressed: Self-Concept, Interpersonal Skills, Growth and Change, Employability Skills, and Decision Making. Three different lessons are provided for each component, and a number of reproducible worksheets are included for student reinforcement of the lessons. The key to using this self-knowledge is in integrating it in such a way that students can't wait to turn on the ignition and get started.

MY FEELINGS ARE OKAY!
Self-Knowledge
"Self-Concept"

OBJECTIVES:

1. Students will be able to share personal experiences that are prompted by pictures of facial expressions that depict various emotions.

2. Students will be able to act out experiences that exemplify those emotions.

3. Students will be able to discuss the importance of validating personal feelings.

SUPPLIES:

Face cards, enlarged and cut apart

Bean bag

PORTFOLIO ENTRY: *Self-Knowledge*, Self-Concept, *"Strengths"* or *"Improve"*

MY FEELINGS ARE OKAY!
Self-Knowledge
"Self-Concept"

LESSON	NOTES
1. **Introduction:** Show students the "faces" cards. Have students give descriptive words for the emotions shown on each face.	
2. **Focus:** Ask the group if they have ever experienced any of these emotions. Briefly, have them share examples.	
3. **Activity:** Scatter the enlarged faces cards on the floor. Ask one student to toss a bean bag at the cards while classmates look away. Ask that student to act out the emotion of the face that was hit by the bean bag by saying three or four sentences that suggest that particular emotion. Have classmates identify the emotion that has been acted out. After three or four skits, ask students to comment on how feelings among individuals can be similar and different. Emphasize that all the experiences shared are personal and okay.	
4. **Closure:** Ask: What did you learn about feelings? What did you learn about yourself? What did you learn about your classmates? Why is it important to respect the feelings of others?	

PASS THE ROLES
Self-Knowledge
"Self-Concept"

OBJECTIVES:

1. Students will be able to describe the difference between a positive and negative self-concept.

2. Students will be able to identify behaviors that enhance a positive self-concept.

3. Students will be able to describe how one's self-concept influences decision making.

SUPPLIES:

Chart paper

Markers

Decision-making situation cards (reproducible provided)

Self-concept cards (reproducible provided)

PORTFOLIO ENTRY: *Self-Knowledge*, Self-Concept, *"Strengths"* or *"Improve"*

PASS THE ROLES
Self-Knowledge
"Self-Concept"

LESSON	NOTES
1. **Introduction:** Ask the following questions and chart the responses. What is a positive self-concept? What is a negative self-concept? How does a person with a positive self-concept act? How does a person with a negative self-concept act?	
2. **Focus:** Explain: Two student volunteers will role play decision-making situations using positive and negative self-concept traits. Observing classmates will analyze the effects of self-concept on the outcomes of important decisions and guess the self-concept of each role-player.	
3. **Activity:** A student volunteer picks a partner and a decision-making card. The partner picks 2 self-concept cards and passes one to the volunteer without looking at it. The decision-making card is read aloud to the class. Role players should act out the scenario for one to three minutes, exemplifying the self-concept traits they have drawn. (Have students refer to the chart for behavior ideas.)	
4. **Closure:** Ask: What did you like about this lesson? What did you learn about self-concept and its effect on decision making? How could the outcomes have been different depending on the self-concept? What did you learn from this lesson?	

DECISION-MAKING SITUATIONS

1. You are a senior and must select a Fine Arts class to complete your graduation requirements. None of them appeal to you. The school counselor has called you to the office.

2. You have been dating the same person for three weeks. The relationship is okay and you'd like to plan a special date without breaking your budget. You ask a friend for help.

3. You begin to notice that your clothes are tight and remarks have been made about your weight by friends. You have little control over the food served at home, but exercise is an option. You choose to discuss it with a teacher who you know recently gave up smoking.

4. You are told by your parents that your mother's annual family reunion will take place on the same weekend as Homecoming Weekend. You've felt pressured to attend the reunion for the past two years, but don't want the hassle of arguing with your mother. You discuss it with your father.

5. One of your friends, who seems to be getting in trouble quite a bit lately, asks you to go to a party this weekend. You've never heard of the person who is having the party. You have to make a decision soon as to whether or not this party is in your plans.

6. You have two days off from school because of teacher conferences. You're trying to figure out what to do with your spare time.

7. You notice that several students in your class have become the object of sexist and racist comments from a group of five students who are generally considered to be "cool." You're trying to decide whether you should do something about it or not.

8. You're feeling pretty stressed out because you have so much to do next week. You have two ball games, a major paper due, two tests, a "bottle drive" for one of your club's fund-raisers, and a canoe trip with your friends on Saturday. How do you deal with it all?

SELF-CONCEPT CARDS

POSITIVE SELF-CONCEPT	**NEGATIVE SELF-CONCEPT**
POSITIVE SELF-CONCEPT	**NEGATIVE SELF-CONCEPT**
POSITIVE SELF-CONCEPT	**NEGATIVE SELF-CONCEPT**
POSITIVE SELF-CONCEPT	**NEGATIVE SELF-CONCEPT**

MIXED MEDIA
Self-Knowledge
"Self-Concept"

OBJECTIVES:

1. Students will be able to use metaphors to describe self-concept.

2. Students will be able to compare the perceptions of parents and peers with their own perceptions of self.

3. Students will be able to further explore aspects of their self-concept.

SUPPLIES:

Mixed Media Student Worksheet

Mixed Media Parent/Guardian Worksheet

PORTFOLIO ENTRY: *Self-Knowledge,* Interpersonal Skills, *"When Others Meet Me"* or *"Competency File"*

MIXED MEDIA
Self-Knowledge
"Self-Concept"

LESSON	NOTES
1. **Introduction:** Tell students that this lesson will allow them to describe themselves by choosing popular media as metaphors.	
2. **Focus:** Ask: What is a metaphor? Use a dictionary if necessary. Have students give examples (i.e. describe your day, your social life, your family life in a metaphor).	
3. **Activity:** Have students individually complete the Mixed Media worksheet. In a group, have students guess the selections of their classmates, defending their choices with facts.	
4. **Closure:** Ask: What did you learn about yourself? Compare your choices with those of your classmates. How do you feel about their choices? How can you use this information in making career choices?	
5. **Follow-up:** Have students ask their parents/guardians to fill in the worksheet. Ask students to discuss the answers with them. In class, have students discuss their parents/guardians' responses and whether they agree/disagree and understand them.	

MIXED MEDIA STUDENT WORKSHEET

Directions: Make choices that best describe how you feel about yourself today. Be able to defend your choices. (Do not share your choices aloud.)

Song title: _____

_____

Video title: _____

_____

Book title: _____

_____

Musical instrument: _____

_____

Make/model car: _____

_____

Parent/Guardian Name _____ **Date** _____

MIXED MEDIA PARENT/GUARDIAN WORKSHEET

Directions: Ask your parents/guardians how they would best describe you using the categories below. Record their answers and reasons.

Song title: _____
_____

Video title: _____
_____

Book title: _____
_____

Musical instrument: _____
_____

Make/model car: _____
_____

TIGER, PERSON, NET
Self-Knowledge
"Interpersonal Skills"

OBJECTIVES:

1. Students will be able to define and apply the concepts of majority and consensus.

2. Students will be able to apply these concepts to a game.

3. Students will be able to discuss their feelings about group consensus.

SUPPLIES:

None

TIGER, PERSON, NET
Self-Knowledge
"Interpersonal Skills"

LESSON	NOTES
1. **Introduction:** Ask students how large groups of people decide on issues. Tell them that the problem with voting is that many people are unhappy with the results. Define majority (winning by one more than half) and consensus (everyone agrees because of compromise and working it out).	
2. **Focus:** Ask students to vote on whether the class' favorite ice cream is vanilla or chocolate. If the majority choice was served, some students wouldn't like it. Have the students decide by consensus. Facilitate compromise and give a time limit to encourage it.	
3. **Activity:** Tell the students that this game relies on consensus. Divide the class into two groups that line up facing each other. Each group must decide quietly by consensus whether to be a tiger (hands near face showing claws), person (bow at waist), or net (weave fingers to look like a net). On the count of three, the groups face each other and show their choices: tiger beats person, person beats net, net beats tiger. If group members are not in consensus and do not show the same action, that group forfeits that turn. There are no prizes, competition is downplayed, and cooperation is encouraged. After two three-game sessions, end.	
4. **Closure:** Ask: How did you feel being part of your group? Why was consensus so important? What problems did your group have? How did you solve them?	

I'VE BEEN A TACT
Self-Knowledge
"Interpersonal Skills"

OBJECTIVES:

1. Students will be able to define tact.

2. Students will be able to identify communication lacking tact.

3. Students will be able to rephrase language to be more tactful.

SUPPLIES:

Dictionary

Chart paper

Markers

I'VE BEEN A TACT
Self-Knowledge
"Interpersonal Skills"

LESSON	NOTES
1. **Introduction:** Ask students for their definition of tact. Use a dictionary for reference.	
2. **Focus:** Ask students to share personal examples of situations that display lack of tact. Chart statements, e.g.: You're so stupid, Dah, Nice hair (sarcastic).	
3. **Activity:** Refer back to definition. In small groups, have students rewrite statements so they display an effective use of tact. Chart tactful statements across from tactless ones.	
4. **Closure:** Ask: Why is being tactful important? What effect does tact have on the receiver of the message? How can being tactful assist you in being more assertive?	

BEST FOOT FORWARD
Self-Knowledge
"Interpersonal Skills"

OBJECTIVES:

1. Students will be able to identify positive interpersonal skills.

2. Students will be able to identify the interpersonal skills they find most challenging.

3. Students will be able to demonstrate how interpersonal skills are used in job situations.

SUPPLIES:

Interpersonal Rating Sheet (provided)

PORTFOLIO ENTRY: *Self-Knowledge,* Personal Qualities or Skills

BEST FOOT FORWARD
Self-Knowledge
"Interpersonal Skills"

LESSON	NOTES

1. **Introduction:** Ask: What do we mean by interpersonal skills? Why are they important?

2. **Focus:** Mention that 75% of employees who lose their jobs do so for lack of interpersonal skills rather than for incompetence. A national commission has identified personal traits most valued by employers. (Refer to SCANS information report in Chapter 2 or "Snap Shot" lesson on page 64. Have students identify qualities and skills which would be most difficult for them to display in a job interview.

3. **Activity:** In groups of four (one applicant, one employer, two observers) have students role play an interview situation based on the job description on the "Interpersonal Rating Sheet." Applicants should "sell" themselves to the employers by convincing them of the high caliber of their interpersonal skills. Observers will score each skill on a score card. Role play for 10 minutes. In a large group, have observers discuss scores.

4. **Closure:** Ask: What are the important lessons that can be learned from this exercise? Why are they important?

INTERPERSONAL RATING SHEET

Directions: From the list of personal traits brainstormed, identify five traits that would be the most difficult to demonstrate in a job interview. List these traits on the scorecard.

Score Card

Directions for observer: Rate each trait during the role play as follows:

Excellent	Good	Adequate	Poor
4	3	2	1

Job Description

Management Training Position: High-volume retail store is now accepting applications for an energetic, dependable, highly motivated individual with excellent people skills. High school graduates preferred; excellent working conditions and benefits; career advancement possibilities. Apply in person.

TRAIT	RATING	EXAMPLES
1.		
2.		
3.		
4.		
5.		

INTERPERSONAL RATING SHEET

Directions: From the list of personal traits brainstormed, identify five traits that would be the most difficult to demonstrate in a job interview. List these traits on the scorecard.

Score Card

Directions for observer: Rate each trait during the role play as follows:

Excellent	Good	Adequate	Poor
4	3	2	1

Job Description

Management Training Position: High volume retail store is now accepting application for an energetic, dependable, highly motivated individual with excellent people skills. High school graduates preferred; excellent working conditions and benefits; career advancement possibilities. Apply in person.

TRAIT	RATING	EXAMPLES
1. **Responsible**	**4**	"People on my paper route say they like how I keep the papers dry when it rains."
2. **Intelligent**	**3**	mentioned good grades
3. **Sense of Humor**	**2**	Nothing funny was said. Didn't talk about how humor is used.
4. **Hard-working**	**4**	"I've had a paper route since I was 12."
5. **"People skills"**	**2**	Not very good eye-contact

OBJECTIVES:

1. Students will be able to identify the six levels of moral development.

2. Students will be able to apply the levels of moral development to role play situations.

3. Students will be able to identify levels of moral development as portrayed in role plays.

SUPPLIES:

Chart paper

Theme cards reproducible

A die

Stages of Moral Development reproducible

PORTFOLIO ENTRY: *Self-Knowledge*, Personal Qualities

LEVELING OUT
Self-Knowledge
"Growth and Change"

LESSON	NOTES
1. **Introduction:** Tell students that as they grow, they develop physically, mentally, and morally. Each phase brings added effort and responsibility.	
2. **Focus:** Hand out the "Stages of Moral Development" reproducible to all students.	
3. **Activity:** In small groups, have students choose a theme card and roll die to determine the moral development level. Give each group 15 minutes to help a volunteer prepare a "soliloquy"—a conversation with self, reflecting on the moral development level that the theme addresses. As each individual presents, have the observers guess the moral development level, giving the reason for the choice.	
4. **Closure:** Ask: Were the levels difficult to guess? Were they difficult to perform? What did you learn from this activity?	

STAGES OF MORAL DEVELOPMENT

Lawrence Kohlberg was a famous psychologist who developed a theory that explains the different levels of reasoning that are used when people must choose between right and wrong. In his six stages of moral development, the lower stages demonstrate immature thinking and reasoning, while the higher stages suggest a more advanced ability to make appropriate moral choices.

The following terms are not Kohlberg's names for the six stages, but they are offered as terms that might be helpful in understanding how each level differs from the other:

STAGE	EXPLANATION
1. Punishment	At this stage, people do what is right to avoid punishment or harm to themselves.
2. Personal	People do what is right because it serves their own needs.
3. Interpersonal	"The Golden Rule" works here: Do unto others as you would have them do to you.
4. Social Conscience	People do what is right to benefit groups to which they belong.
5. Human Rights	At this stage, people have an appreciation for why rules and laws are needed to protect people's rights and to make the world a better place.
6. Ethical	People who are ethical do what is right because they know it is the best way to act and they don't need rules or laws to help them decide.

THEME CARDS

Directions: Cut out each theme and place in a container for student selection.

PEER PRESSURE: substance use or shoplifting	CHEATING: at school or at work
RESPONSIBLE BEHAVIOR: in a car, at home, or on the school bus	QUITTING: on the job or on a team
BULLYING: at home, at school, or on the job	ATTENTION, SEEKING BEHAVIOR: at school, at home, or with friends
REPORTING RULE VIOLATIONS: at school, at home, or in the community	HARASSMENT: at school, on a team, or, social situation

MILESTONES
Self-Knowledge
"Growth and Change"

OBJECTIVES:

1. Students will be able to identify major developmental milestones.

2. Students will be able to recognize significant developmental time frames.

3. Students will be able to draw personal conclusions about the impact of growth and change.

SUPPLIES:

Chalkboard or chart paper

10′ butcher paper

3 × 5 cards (five for each student)

Masking tape

PORTFOLIO ENTRY: *Self-Knowledge, Things I've Learned about Self*

MILESTONES
Self-Knowledge
"Growth and Change"

LESSON	NOTES
1. **Introduction:** Ask students if they've ever developed a timeline in social studies or history classes. What was the purpose of the timeline?	
2. **Focus:** Explain that this lesson is very much like the timeline, because it asks them to record significant dates in their personal lives. This one, however, will also go into the future, as they think about important milestones they anticipate.	
3. **Activity:** Ask students to brainstorm various milestones in their lives (e.g., lose first tooth, religious celebrations, have grandchildren etc.). Chart the list and explain that students will be placing the milestones on the butcher sheet on the wall. (NOTE: Butcher sheet should be blocked off in 10-year segments prior to the class meeting.) Pass out five index cards to each student. Have them individually choose five milestones, print one on each card, and place the cards in the appropriate place on the milestone timeline. (Student placement will differ.) Share the different milestones on the timeline.	
4. **Closure:** Ask students: How do your personal milestones compare with those of your classmates? What elements need to be considered? What does the milestone timeline tell you about your class? Is there consensus about the location of the cards? How can you use this information in making career choices?	
5. **Follow-up:** Do the "Dear Baby" lesson on page 54. Check computer software for additional timeline formats and applications. Have students explain this activity to their parents and get feedback.	

OBJECTIVES:

1. Students will be able to recognize their own major personal developmental milestones.

2. Students will be able to apply lessons learned from the past to assist in planning for the future.

3. Students will be able to describe their appreciation for the lessons learned in a personal history.

SUPPLIES:

None

"DEAR BABY"
Self-Knowledge
"Growth and Change"

LESSON	NOTES

1. **Introduction:** Ask students to reflect on classes where timelines were used. What would be the benefit of creating a personal timeline?

2. **Focus:** Refer to milestone chart used in previous lesson. Review the similarities and differences of individual students.

3. **Activity:** Have students create their own personal milestone worksheet, adding any additional information that may not have been included before (e.g., death of a loved one, financial problems, etc.). Have students share their responses in small groups.

   As a homework assignment, have students compose a letter to their unborn child. After the introduction "Dear Baby," the piece should include the following:

   a) highlights of their lives

   b) lessons learned from their life experiences

   c) future personal plans

   d) dreams for the child's future

4. **Closure:** Prior to sharing the letters, have students reflect on the difficulty of the assignment. Ask: Why was it difficult? Why was it easy? Why was the assignment given? Have volunteers share their letters and discuss the contents as time allows.

OBJECTIVES:

1. Students will be able to explain the six steps in problem solving.

2. Students will be able to apply these steps to work-related scenarios.

3. Students will be able to identify appropriate work-related decisions.

SUPPLIES:

"Hired or Fired" situation cards

"Hired or Fired" employee decision cards

HIRED OR FIRED
Self-Knowledge
"Employability Skills"

LESSON	NOTES
1. **Introduction:** List the six steps of problem solving: 1. Say the problem; 2. Brainstorm all possible solutions; 3. Consider the consequences; 4. Choose; 5. Act; and 6. Evaluate. Have students comment on the importance of each step. Discuss the importance of the steps being followed in order.	
2. **Focus:** Tell students that they will be divided into small groups to solve problems that are work-related. They should follow the six steps of problem solving and then decide whether the individual making the decision should be hired or fired from the job.	
3. **Activity:** Divide students into small groups and pass out a Situation Card to each group. Give groups 10 minutes to work through the 6 problem solving steps. When each group has reached consensus, give them the Employee Decision Card that corresponds to their situation. The group then decides if the employee should be rehired or fired. Discuss each group's problem-solving situation and the final decision.	
4. **Closure:** Ask: What have you learned from this lesson? How does this lesson prepare you for the world of work? How would it feel to make these decisions as an employer?	

HIRED OR FIRED
SITUATION CARDS

1. Jesse has a regular babysitting job for 2 children under the age of 6. The Montgomerys count on her to watch their children from 7-10 p.m. every Thursday while they attend Adult Education classes. Jessie's best friend calls late in the afternoon and says she just got 2 tickets for a rock concert that night. What should she do?

2. Mark has been doing errands for the past 4 years for the Smiths, an older couple in the neighborhood. With each year his jobs have increased in responsibility and pay. His jobs have gone from raking the yard and taking out trash to cleaning the cellar and paying the bills. One afternoon, Mark discovers that Mr. Smith has overpaid him $100. What should he do?

3. Harold has agreed to feed and walk the Pinsons' dog while they are on vacation. Although he has fed him each day, he left him out to roam the street one night. The canine patrol picked up the dog overnight. Harold happens to be at the Pinsons' house when the sheriff delivers the notice that they must pay a fine. What should he do?

4. Kesha was hired by the Barkowski family to mow their lawn while they were away for three weeks. She waited until two days before they were due home, and by then the grass was so long that the lawn mower kept stalling when she mowed it. What should she do?

5. Marleena got a job at an ice cream stand for the summer. Her friends would come to visit her while she was working and ask for free ice cream. What should she do?

6. Rico was hired as a dishwasher at a local restaurant. He would come home from work exhausted, complaining about the hot, steamy working conditions, all the garbage people would leave on their plates, and the backaches he got from bending over the sink and dishwasher. He really doesn't feel like going to work today. What should he do?

HIRED OR FIRED EMPLOYEE DECISION CARDS

1. Jesse asks her older sister to fill in for her and checks it out with the Montgomerys. They say it's fine.

2. Mark takes the cash and never tells the Smiths.

3. Harold tells the Pinsons about the situation. He admits to them that he wouldn't be able to pay the fine. He asks if he could do other jobs to earn the money to pay the fine.

4. Kesha kept mowing the lawn and finally finished it before the Barkowski family came home. However, she didn't find the time to rake up all the clumps of grass that were left on the lawn.

5. Marleena told her friends that if she gave all of them free ice cream then the profits would come out of her paycheck.

6. Rico stayed home. The employer called and Rico told him that he didn't want to work there anymore.

HEARING AIDS
Self-Knowledge
"Employability Skills"

OBJECTIVES:

1. Students will be able to identify situations in which they were not good listeners.

2. Students will be able to identify positive listening skills.

3. Students will be able to create appropriate listening skills in work situation role plays.

SUPPLIES:

Role Play situations handout.

HEARING AIDS
Self-Knowledge
"Employability Skills"

LESSON	NOTES
1. **Introduction:** Ask students to give examples of times when it was obvious that people were not listening to what they were saying.	
2. **Focus:** Inform students that listening skills are not only highly valued but are the most used communication skill on the job. Brainstorm positive listening skills, focusing on how students like to be listened to (e.g., eye contact, ask good questions, respond to details).	
3. **Activity:** Pass out "Role Play Situations" to students. In groups of three, with one student acting as the observer, role play work-related situations for five minutes. Have observers provide feedback. If time allows, switch roles.	
4. **Closure:** Ask: What was difficult about the situations? Easy? What are some important messages that can be applied to the world of work? How can you practice these on a daily basis?	

ROLE PLAY SITUATIONS

Employer with good listening skills responding to an employee who is late for the second time this week.

Employer with good listening skills who responds to an employee who is feeling overwhelmed by a particular work task.

Employee with good listening skills responding to an employer who is frustrated with the upkeep of the outside of the building.

Employee with good listening skills responding to an employer who wants employees to take a more active role in managing the business.

Employer with good listening skills responding to an employee who has had problems at home.

Employee with good listening skills responding to customer complaints.

SAMPLE ROLE PLAYS

Directions: If students have difficulty creating role play situations, these examples may be used to illustrate the kinds of employer-employee exchanges that could be developed.

Employee:	"I know this is the second time that I've been late this week. The first time I had a flat tire and this time they were stopping traffic for some road construction work."
Employer (good listener):	"I understand that you've had some reasons for being late that were beyond your control. Do you think there could have been a better way of handling the situation?"
Employer:	"This place is a pig sty! People driving by must think we don't even care what this place looks like. Doesn't anyone ever pick up anything on the sidewalk outside?"
Employee (good listener):	"I hear you, Mr. B. You want us to pick up the litter outside so the place looks better for customers."
Disgruntled Customer:	"I'm never coming back to this store. This piece of junk was broken when I took it out of the box. How do you expect to stay in business selling this kind of garbage?"
Employee (good listener):	"I can see that you're upset. It's frustrating when you buy something and you open it up and it's broken. Let me take care of it for you."

OBJECTIVES:

1. Students will be able to discuss the need for personal competencies as successful students.

2. Students will be able to discuss the need for personal competencies as workers.

3. Students will be able to assess their need to develop these competencies as future workers.

SUPPLIES:

"Snap Shot Interview" worksheet

A list of community role models (provided)

SNAP SHOT
Self-Knowledge
"Employability Skills"

LESSON	NOTES
1. **Introduction:** Tell students that there are 10 competencies that employers agree are important for successful employees to exhibit. (See "Snap Shot Interview" worksheet.)	
2. **Focus:** Ask students to define each trait. Discuss the importance of each as it applies to them as students. You may want to assign this prior to class.	
3. **Activity:** In class, discuss the interview process (e.g., call, set appointment, explain assignment, etc.). Have students conduct interviews with community role models. Allow a number of days for this to be completed. Have each student share one story or "snap shot" that was particularly memorable that showed the development of a competency in the interviewee.	
4. **Closure:** Ask: What did you learn about yourself? What did you learn about developing these competencies? Which will be the most difficult for you to develop?	
5. **Follow-up:** Assign a reaction paper that addresses how students can better develop their own personal competencies.	

SNAP SHOT INTERVIEW WORKSHEET

Ask community interviewees how they developed some of the traits and skills that make them successful in their personal and professional lives. Ask them to share specific experiences that illustrate how they learned about these traits and skills, and how they use them in their work. (Use additional paper if necessary.)

Interviewee: _____

Professional Title: _____

_____

1. RESPONSIBILITY
   a. growing up: _____

   _____

   b. on the job: _____

   _____

2. SELF-ESTEEM
   a. growing up: _____

   _____

   b. on the job: _____

   _____

3. SOCIABILITY
   a. growing up: _____

   _____

   b. on the job: _____

   _____

4. INTEGRITY/HONESTY
   a. growing up: _____

   _____

   b. on the job: _____

   _____

SNAP SHOT INTERVIEW WORKSHEET
(CONTINUED)

5. COOPERATION

    a. growing up: _____

    _____

    b. on the job: _____

    _____

6. SELF-MANAGEMENT

    a. growing up: _____

    _____

    b. on the job: _____

    _____

7. NEGOTIATING

    a. growing up: _____

    _____

    b. on the job: _____

    _____

8. PROBLEM SOLVING

    a. growing up: _____

    _____

    b. on the job: _____

    _____

9. LISTENING

    a. growing up: _____

    _____

    b. on the job: _____

    _____

10. SPEAKING

    a. growing up: _____

    _____

    b. on the job: _____

    _____

MONARCH/MAJORITY/MAYHEM
Self-Knowledge
"Decision Making"

OBJECTIVES:

1. Students will be able to define the terms monarchy, majority, and mayhem.

2. Students will be able to make a group decision using these methods.

3. Students will be able to evaluate each method for efficiency and group satisfaction.

SUPPLIES:

Dictionary

MONARCHY/MAJORITY/MAYHEM
Self-Knowledge
"Decision Making"

LESSON	NOTES
1. **Introduction:** Tell students that this lesson will be an exercise in group decision making.	
2. **Focus:** Ask students to define the terms monarchy, majority, and mayhem and how they would be applied to group decision making. Ask if there is any other method of making group decisions. (Consensus might be suggested.)	
3. **Activity:** In small groups, have students make a group decision on their favorite color (or dessert, animal, song, etc.) using the three previously discussed methods (monarchy, majority, mayhem). Give 3-5 minutes for each method.	
4. **Closure:** In large group ask: How time-efficient was each method? How involved were the group members? How did group members react to each decision? Were group members satisfied with each decision? Which method do you personally prefer?	
5. **Follow-up:** Use the same process and have students decide by consensus. Discuss the challenges of using this method.	
6. **Enrichment:** Have students research autocratic, democratic, and *laissez faire* leadership styles.	

SNAP DRAGON
Self-Knowledge
"Decision Making"

OBJECTIVES:

1. Students will be able to identify difficult, unexpected decisions.

2. Students will be able to identify the skills necessary to make good "snap" decisions.

3. Students will be able to apply these skills to life situations.

SUPPLIES:

Chart paper and markers

or

Chalkboard and chalk

SNAP DRAGON
Self-Knowledge
"Decision Making"

LESSON	NOTES
1. **Introduction:** Ask students to describe difficult decisions they have to make that they don't usually expect. (Examples unexpected invitation to a dance, competition for academic honor, unexpected job offer that conflicts with a social event.)	
2. **Focus:** Ask students what skills are necessary to make good "snap" decisions. (See "Hired or Fired" lesson on page 56.) Chart for all to see.	
3. **Activity:** Ask students to identify the skills that will be needed to make "snap" decisions. Have them decide upon the procedures they would follow if they awoke one morning and found a dragon in the yard. (This may be done individually, in pairs, or in small groups.) Give 10 minutes. Share with the large group.	
4. **Closure:** Ask: What skills did you use to make this decision? How did the decisions vary? Why? Did you hear other decisions that were better than yours? What other kinds of decisions might require these skills?	

STYLE SHOW
Self-Knowledge
"Decision Making"

OBJECTIVES:

1. Students will be able to apply creative problem-solving skills.

2. Students will be able to complete a small group project with all members participating and cooperating.

3. Students will be able to verbalize the individual and group decision-making skills necessary to complete the project.

SUPPLIES:

Newspapers

Staplers

Staples

STYLE SHOW
Self-Knowledge
"Decision Making"

LESSON	NOTES
1. **Introduction:** Ask the students to divide themselves into small groups of about four or five with fairly equal numbers of girls and boys. Optional: Identify one person in each group to observe and note the decision-making process.	
2. **Focus:** Explain that the activity will involve choosing a "model," deciding on a style theme, and creating a recognizable costume out of newspapers and staples. Students are encouraged to note the group decision-making skills necessary to complete the project.	
3. **Activity:** Give students the supplies and about 20 minutes to complete the activity. As the models display each group's creation, have students in the other groups guess the theme of the costume.	
4. **Closure:** Ask: What decisions did your group have to make? Describe what happened. What is the importance of this lesson? What did you learn about group decision making? How might these skills be applicable in job situations?	

CHAPTER FIVE

Nice Set o' Wheels

Lessons to Help Students Examine Life Roles

Nothing makes for a smooth ride like a great set of tires. The tires and wheels create the support for the vehicle that will act as a buffer between the rough road and the car's occupants. The wheels are connected to the frame of the car, serving as the means for turning the car in various directions, and absorbing many of the bumps and stressors that seem to appear along the road. The wheels need to be properly aligned if the car is to respond well and stay on a steady course without veering too far to the left or right. The tires cover the wheels and help provide the proper traction both for creating a comfortable ride and for moving the vehicle through slippery spots. To give this kind of ride, the tires need to be well balanced and have just the right amount of inflation. The quality of the ride is almost always seen in the quality of the tire.

A student's career journey deserves and requires a strong foundation—a support system that can help the student make the proper turns, weather the rough spots, and maintain a steady course. Students need to understand the impact of family, friends, and other influences in their lives that contribute to their beliefs, aspirations, and sense of meaningfulness. Just as the wheels need to be aligned and the tires balanced, students need to have a sense of the rules they operate by and what creates balance in their lives. In exploring their life roles, some students will find it reaffirming to note the cultural and sociological influences on their development. For other students, this exploration may reveal imbalances that need to be corrected if they are to avoid a rough journey. Of course, when it comes to inflation, we want students to surround themselves with a support system that helps them build a healthy self-esteem without becoming overly inflated. Some of that inflation can come from others, but a significant amount of the pressure needs to come from within, as students internalize the important messages and guidelines that shape their decision making and goal setting. Remember, a minimal amount of pressure and an adequate amount of inflation is a good thing. Students need to have a sense of where that good pressure and good inflation come from. They also need to know how to use that knowledge to create balance in their lives and to support them on their career journeys.

In this chapter, five different components of one's Life Roles are explored: Cultural Heritage, Understanding Roles, Acceptance of Others, Assertiveness Skills, and the Use of Leisure Time. The three lessons and activities under each component allow students to explore their own life roles, while they also nurture tolerance and acceptance of others' life roles. This set of lessons is particularly helpful in including families in the career exploration process. Once again, the challenge for educators is to help students reflect on these lessons and find ways to integrate their insights within the career awareness–exploration–preparation framework.

DANGLING CONVERSATIONS
Life Roles
"Cultural Heritage"

OBJECTIVES:

1. Students will be able to define the term "culture."

2. Students will be able to create mobiles that reflect their personal cultures.

3. Students will be able to appreciate the personal cultures of their classmates by suggesting ways that personal culture can be included in conversation.

SUPPLIES:

Coat hangers

Yarn

String

Dictionary

PORTFOLIO ENTRY: *Life Roles*, Acceptance of Self and Others, *"Heritage Influence," "Accepting Others"*

DANGLING CONVERSATIONS
Life Roles
"Cultural Heritage"

LESSON	NOTES
1. **Introduction:** Have students define and discuss the term "culture." Explain that culture is reflected not only in national and community norms, but also in family and personal life choices.	
2. **Focus:** Ask how your personal culture is reflected in everyday life.	
3. **Activity:** Ask students to create mobiles that reflect their own personal cultures. Items may include personal belongings, such as books, music, favorite possessions, etc. Display the mobiles and give students the opportunity to explain them to the class. Encourage questions.	
4. **Closure:** Ask: What did you like about this assignment? What did you learn about the personal cultures of your classmates? How can we show respect for personal culture? How can this activity influence your personal conversations?	

HIDDEN TREASURES
Life Roles
"Cultural Heritage"

OBJECTIVES:

1. Students will be able to recognize subtle family traditions.

2. Students will be able to discuss their personal choices for continuing an established tradition.

3. Students will be able to recognize the challenges of maintaining traditions when they establish new permanent relationships.

SUPPLIES:

"Hidden Treasure" worksheet

SPECIAL NOTE:

Some students may lack any traditions or special memories of family rituals. Let them know that it is okay if they do not have many items for their worksheet. Help them learn from others and focus on the "treasures" they would like to create for their families in the future.

PORTFOLIO ENTRY: *Life Roles,* Acceptance of Others, *"Cultural Heritage"*

HIDDEN TREASURES
Life Roles
"Cultural Heritage"

LESSON	NOTES
1. **Introduction:** Tell students that there are many traditions that are typically celebrated by families. However, there are far more subtle traditions that make up the true culture of the family.	
2. **Focus:** Refer students to "Hidden Treasures" worksheet. Briefly discuss the categories and, depending on student input, make additions. Ask students to give very specific examples in each category as they do the worksheet, with input from their parents and siblings.	
3. **Activity:** In groups of three, have individual students share three "hidden treasures" they intend to carry on as adults. Have them defend and explain why each is important to them.	
4. **Closure:** In large groups ask: What is the significance of subtle traditions in people's lives? Which traditions could harmonize with yours? What challenges would you anticipate in compromising traditions? What new traditions did you hear that you'd enjoy incorporating into your traditions? What significance does this lesson have for future life decisions?	

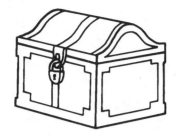

HIDDEN TREASURES
WORKSHEET

Directions: Brainstorm the more subtle traditions that define how your family creates special meaning in your lives. Be specific.

1. MEALTIMES (breakfast–on–the–run, formal Sunday meals)

   _____

   _____

2. VACATIONS (camping, ski trips)

   _____

   _____

3. LEISURE (competitive games, attendance at sporting events with relatives)

   _____

   _____

4. SPECIAL EVENTS (special recognition, nontraditional holiday activities)

   _____

   _____

5. FAMILY TIES (family reunions, anniversaries)

   _____

   _____

6. DAILY ROUTINES (watching the news, exercise at a special time)

   _____

   _____

7. COMMUNICATION (bedtime stories, affectionate names)

   _____

   _____

8. RELIGION (church activities, daily devotions)

   _____

   _____

9. OTHER:

   _____

   _____

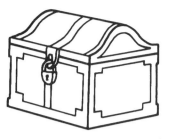

HIDDEN TREASURES WORKSHEET

Directions: Brainstorm the more subtle traditions that define how your family creates special meaning in your lives. Be specific.

1. MEALTIMES (breakfast–on–the–run, formal Sunday meals)

   We hold hands and everybody says one thing they're thankful for—sorta like grace.

   _____

2. VACATIONS (camping, ski trips)

   We always sing in the car on our trips.

   _____

3. LEISURE (competitive games, attendance at sporting events with relatives)

   Family volleyball games at family gatherings.

   We always have a small garden.

4. SPECIAL EVENTS (special recognition, nontraditional holiday activities)

   We get to open one small present on the morning of our birthdays.

   Holidays always have a big meal.

5. FAMILY TIES (family reunions, anniversaries)

   Our family gets together every summer for a lobster/clambake.

   _____

6. DAILY ROUTINES (watching the news, exercise at a special time)

   Dad fixes breakfast and lunch for everybody while they get ready for school or work.

   _____

7. COMMUNICATION (bedtime stories, affectionate names)

   Dad always reads "Happy Birthday to You" by Dr. Seuss on everybody's birthday (or does this go

   under special events?) Weekly telephone conversations with close relatives.

8. RELIGION (church activities, daily devotions)

   Taught that religion is your way of life.

   _____

9. OTHER:

   Mom bakes a special cake for us on our birthdays that her mom baked for her when she grew up.

   We always add an extra candle for good luck or to grow on.

A STORY THAT MATTERS
Life Roles
"Cultural Heritage"

OBJECTIVES:

1. Students will be able to explore parental involvement in their life development.

2. Students will be able to compare and contrast their perceptions with those of their parents.

3. Students will be able to produce a written piece that incorporates their parents' messages into a meaningful personal "story that matters."

SUPPLIES:

"A Story That Matters" student worksheet

"A Story That Matters" parent/quardian worksheet

PORTFOLIO ENTRY: *Life Roles,* Competency Skills, *"Evolving Life Roles"*

A STORY THAT MATTERS
Life Roles
"Cultural Heritage"

LESSON	NOTES
1. **Introduction:** Share a personal anecdote that reflects an important message learned from a parent or significant adult. Explain whether this message came by direct instruction or through innuendo.	
2. **Focus:** Refer to the student worksheet. Briefly discuss the items, have the students fill them out, then share in pairs. Assign the parent worksheet for homework.	
3. **Activity:** Discuss the differences in the answers on the surveys. Assign students a written piece that incorporates their parents' or guardians' messages into a meaningful personal "story that matters." Explain that even though the messages may be **very** different, lessons can be learned through the experience (Example: Mother says to work for money, while Father says to work for enjoyment. The student learns that there are various ways that people view working.) Have students share their completed pieces in small groups.	
4. **Closure:** Ask: What did you learn from this lesson? What did you learn about your classmates from this lesson? Were any parent/guardian messages similar? How different were they from yours? Were yours similar to those of your classmates? How can this lesson be applied to future life choices?	

A STORY THAT MATTERS
(STUDENT WORKSHEET)

Directions for students in class: Explain what message each parent or guardian gives you on the following topics:

MARRIAGE

_____

_____

FRIENDS

_____

FAMILY

_____

_____

WORK

_____

LEISURE

_____

_____

SPIRITUALITY

_____

_____

POLITICS

_____

_____

OTHER

_____

_____

A STORY THAT MATTERS
(PARENT/GUARDIAN WORKSHEET)

Directions for parents/guardians: What "words of wisdom" do you want to give your children on the following topics? (Although we encourage discussion after the completion of this worksheet, please do not discuss it prior to filling it out.)

MARRIAGE _____

_____

FRIENDS _____

_____

FAMILY _____

_____

WORK _____

_____

LEISURE _____

_____

SPIRITUALITY _____

_____

POLITICS _____

_____

OTHER _____

_____

LIFE'S A PUZZLE
Life Roles
"Understanding Roles"

OBJECTIVES:

1. Students will be able to identify the relative importance of current life roles.

2. Students will be able to visualize the importance of each role in their lives.

3. Students will be able to compare their perspectives with those of their classmates and significant adults.

SUPPLIES:

1 piece of construction paper per student

Scissors (optional)

Index cards

PORTFOLIO ENTRY: *Life Roles,* Competency Skills, *"Interrelationships in Life Roles"*

LIFE'S A PUZZLE
Life Roles
"Understanding Roles"

LESSON	NOTES
1. **Introduction:** Tell students that the lesson will address the varying roles that one plays in everyday life.	
2. **Focus:** Ask students to brainstorm the roles that they play daily. Examples might include: son/daughter, student, church member, ball player, etc. As students share, record each role on an index card. Have students sort the cards into six categories and label each (e.g., FAMILY MEMBER, FRIEND, LEISURITE, WORKER, COMMUNITY MEMBER, RELIGIOUS/SPIRITUAL BEING.	
3. **Activity:** When students have brainstormed extensively, label the groups. With each student supplied with a piece of construction paper, have them cut or tear six pieces that represent the amount of time they spend filling each role on a weekly basis. Have students label and compare their pieces. Take a poll as to which roles are the biggest and smallest.	
4. **Closure:** Ask: What was the purpose of this activity? Why was it important? How did you compare with your peers? What similarities/differences did you notice? Do you think your other family members would view your roles differently? How would you view the roles of other family members?	
5. **Follow–up:** Suggest to students that they do the same activity with a sibling or parent.	

OBJECTIVES:

1. Students will be able to recognize typical roles that classmates play in group decision making through a role play.

2. Students will be able to recognize the value of diversity of roles in group decision making.

3. Students will be able to identify the roles that they typically play in group decision making.

SUPPLIES:

"Role Play Cards" reproducibles

PORTFOLIO ENTRY: *Life Roles,* Competency Skills, *"Life Roles Affected by Others"*

DOING IT "OUR" WAY
Life Roles
"Understanding Roles"

LESSON	NOTES
1. **Introduction:** Tell students that the lesson involves excellent observation skills. Tell them that a small group will problem solve while role playing. As observers, the other students will be asked to describe and name the roles they observed.	
2. **Focus:** Ask for volunteers and assign roles. (See Role Play Cards reproducible.) Conference privately with role players so they understand their roles.	

3. **Activity:** Have role players sit in a small circle surrounded by the observers in a larger circle. Assign the question: Your class must raise $2,000 for a class trip in three months. Decide how to raise the money without asking for personal student donations.

OR

Your class has been asked to do a community service project to help a nonprofit organization. Decide what to do.

4. **Closure:** Ask: What did you learn about group decision making? What did you learn about the roles people assume in groups? What are the problems encountered by the group because of the roles? Do you recognize yourself in the group? Which role would you find difficult to play?

DOING IT "OUR" WAY
ROLE PLAY CARDS

Teacher note: Choose volunteers to play roles that are different from their typical style of group participation. You may also start with three or four players and then add the others at intervals. You also have the option of passing out the roles without the titles. Have students create names for the roles. All roles need not be used in the same role play.

Directions: Cut out each role and pass to individual students.

ORGANIZER—a person who tries to organize everyone and works out all the details.

SILENT TYPE—a person who rarely shares any ideas unless he/she is pressured.

SOCIALIZER—a person who tries to get everyone to participate.

NEGATIVE ONE—a person who dislikes every idea and rarely agrees on anything.

DOING IT "OUR" WAY
ROLE PLAY CARDS
(CONTINUED)

BOSS—a person who immediately takes charge and thinks he/she needs to tell everyone what to do.

IDEA PERSON—a person who always comes up with great and sometimes unusual ideas.

CLOWN—a person who makes a joke about everything that is said, talks out of turn, gets people off topic, and has a hard time being serious.

MONOPOLIZER—a person who constantly wants to share ideas, is always talking, and insists that his/her ideas be considered.

COMPROMISER—a person who tries to appreciate all ideas and blend them to create one that is acceptable to all.

BE YOURSELF—participate when you have an idea and feel comfortable.

Life Roles
"Understanding Roles"

OBJECTIVES:

1. Students will be able to brainstorm sex-stereotypical roles.

2. Students will be able to appreciate the value of personal choice in selecting a career.

3. Students will be able to produce a written piece that incorporates gender issues in career choices.

SUPPLIES:

Chart paper

Markers

PORTFOLIO ENTRY: *Life Roles,* Competency Skills, *"Roles Affected by Others"* or *"Gender Roles"*

A DIFFERENT POINT OF VIEW
Life Roles
"Understanding Roles"

LESSON	NOTES

1. **Introduction:** Ask students to brainstorm occupations that are typically held by a certain gender. Discuss the reasons why this may still exist for some professions.

2. **Focus:** Ask students to discuss the activities that make up a particular job and the elements that may make it seem inappropriate for a certain gender. (Examples: secretary; construction worker; hairdresser; plumber.)

3. **Activity:** Mention to students that if fully financed educational opportunities were offered to students who pursue nontraditional occupations, perhaps the general trend would reverse itself. Assignment: Write a letter to a benefactor who will finance a $10,000 scholarship to a student pursuing a nontraditional career. Emphasize the personal challenge, the benefit to society, the need for financing, the personal rewards, the individual commitment, the importance of non-traditional role models and the importance of public support of such ventures. Share the pieces in small groups.

4. **Closure:** Ask: What was the value of this lesson? Who might benefit from this exercise? How would your parents react to this assignment? Do you know of any such benefactor? Where could you find out?

5. **Follow-up:** Invite guest speakers who are in nontraditional careers to speak to the class about their occupations, challenges, and rewards.

LABEL TALK
Life Roles
"Acceptance of Others"

OBJECTIVES:

1. Students will be able to recognize how labels promote expectations about behavior.

2. Students will be able to personalize how labels limit their understanding of others.

3. Students will be able to identify situations where labeling may limit their self-development.

SUPPLIES:

Chart paper

Markers

PORTFOLIO ENTRY: *Life Roles,* Competency Skills, *"Influences on Gender Roles" or "Stereotyping and Bias"*

LABEL TALK
Life Roles
"Acceptance of Others"

LESSON	NOTES
1. **Introduction:** Tell students that the topic of the lesson is "labels." Ask them to discuss how labels are assigned to individuals. Brainstorm typical peer labels.	
2. **Focus:** Tell students that people are often labeled inappropriately. Ask for volunteers who will wear "labels" on their foreheads without knowing what the label is.	
3. **Activity:** Assign volunteers the following labels: joker, clothes horse, jock, genius, teacher's pet, scapegoat. The class will then discuss the topic of raising $1,000 for a class trip. Individuals should respond to the suggestions of the volunteers according to their labels. Basically, they will be giving the volunteers hints about their labels. After 10 minutes of discussion, ask volunteers to guess their labels and indicate what led them to their choices. Ask volunteers to share their feelings about how people treated them during the discussion time.	
4. **Closure:** Ask: How do labels limit our understanding of others? How difficult is it to change a label? How can that be accomplished? How can labels limit your self-development and that of others?	

DEAR EDITOR
Life Roles
"Acceptance of Others"

OBJECTIVES:

1. Students will be able to define tolerance.

2. Students will be able to give examples of tolerant acts and see how the lesson applies to their lives.

3. Students will be able to apply critical thinking skills to critique published expressions of opinion.

SUPPLIES:

Letters to the editor from the local newspaper (a different letter for each small group)

"Dear Editor" worksheet

PORTFOLIO ENTRY: *Life Roles,* Competency Skills, *"Life Roles Affected by Others"*

DEAR EDITOR
Life Roles
"Acceptance of Others"

LESSON	NOTES
1. **Introduction:** Tell students that the lesson will explore tolerance (a dictionary may be needed).	
2. **Focus:** Ask students to give examples of tolerant acts. Encourage them to give examples from their own lives, rather than from world events.	
3. **Activity:** In small groups, have students read and discuss copies of three different letters to the editor from a local newspaper. After 10 minutes, pass out the worksheet and ask students to individually critique each letter. When that is complete, have each group tally the scores to see which letter ranks highest.	
4. **Closure:** Ask: What is your definition of tolerance? Where would its use be most helpful in your life? How can individuals practice tolerance daily? How would tolerance improve the quality of life in the school community?	
5. **Follow-up:** Suggest that students write letters to the editor about tolerance issues in the community.	

DEAR EDITOR WORKSHEET

Directions: Rank your "letter to the editor" as follows:

4	**3**	**2**	**1**
superior	adequate	mediocre	inappropriate

Letter to Editor By-line: _____

1. TOLERANT _____

_____

_____

2. BASED ON FACT_____

_____

_____

3. EXPRESSED EMOTION _____

_____

_____

4. APPROPRIATE WRITING SKILLS _____

_____

_____

5. OFFERS ALTERNATIVE ACTIONS_____

_____

_____

DEAR EDITOR WORKSHEET

Directions: Rank your "letter to the editor" as follows:

4   **3**   **②**   **1**
superior   adequate   mediocre   inappropriate

Letter to Editor By-line: <u>Turnpike Widening Still Controversial</u>

1. TOLERANT <u>Author was not tolerant of change. "Do we want more curio shops and flea</u> <u>markets? More noise and fewer available sites at campgrounds? Have we not had enough?"</u>

2. BASED ON FACT <u>Used examples from another state—more observation than fact.</u> <u>Did not provide any facts to support arguments.</u>

3. EXPRESSED EMOTION <u>Appealed to "mother nature" emotional link. "Mother nature has</u> <u>struck back at overused and undermanaged roads and campgrounds and washed them away."</u>

4. APPROPRIATE WRITING SKILLS <u>Good skills. Interesting writing style. Uses</u> <u>examples to make a point.</u>

5. OFFERS ALTERNATIVE ACTIONS <u>The alternative is to keep things the way they are.</u>

DRAWING THE LINE
Life Roles
"Acceptance of Others"

OBJECTIVES:

1. Students will be able to identify behaviors that are bothersome.

2. Students will be able to decide when bothersome behavior needs to be addressed.

3. Students will be able to identify skills that tactfully address bothersome behavior.

SUPPLIES:

Chart paper or oak tag strips

PORTFOLIO ENTRY: *Life Roles,* Competency Skills, *"Relationship with Others"*

DRAWING THE LINE
Life Roles
"Acceptance of Others"

LESSON	NOTES
1. **Introduction:** Tell students that the lesson will address bothersome behaviors.	
2. **Focus:** Have students brainstorm examples of bothersome behaviors (e.g., messiness, poor manners, borrowing without asking, tapping pencil). As students brainstorm, write the items on individual strips of chart paper or oak tag.	
3. **Activity:** Define the terms "invasive" and "noninvasive" as they relate to bothersome behavior. Have students categorize the brainstormed list as invasive or noninvasive. When that is complete, ask for suggestions on how to address invasive behavior. Chart examples (e.g., politely ask the person to stop, use humor, gentle reminders).	
4. **Closure:** Ask: What did you learn from this lesson? Why is it important? What consequences can you predict? How difficult is it to address bothersome behavior?	
5. **Follow-up:** From the brainstormed list of activities to address invasive behavior, role play situations for students to practice.	

VOWEL PLAY
Life Roles
"Assertiveness Skills"

OBJECTIVES:

1. Students will be able to identify reactions and feelings as they respond to conflict.

2. Students will be able to label their reactions and feelings into five categories.

3. Students will be able to identify their most frequent use of each response to conflict.

SUPPLIES:

"Vowel Play" worksheet

VOWEL PLAY
Life Roles
"Assertiveness Skills"

LESSON	NOTES
1. **Introduction:** Tell students that the lesson will focus on conflict, and how they may typically respond to it.	
2. **Focus:** Pass out the worksheets and ask students to answer the two sections entitled, "HOW I REACT," and "HOW I FEEL." After eight minutes, have students share their responses in a large group setting.	
3. **Activity:** As students share, designate each response with the following letters based on the content:	

A—angry and aggressive

E—evading the conflict, ignoring or walking away

I—an "I" response, "I feel..."

O—an opening for the other person, "How do you feel?"

U—a unifying statement, "We can work it out together."

Encourage the students to figure out what the letters indicate. Have them count the number of each response.

4. **Closure:** Ask: What does this tell you about your responses to conflict situations? Are you satisfied with these responses? Do your responses make the conflict better or worse? What responses might be more effective?

5. **Follow-up:** Ask students to give examples of alternative methods to respond to their conflict situations that might be more effective.

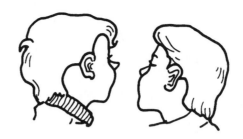

VOWEL PLAY WORKSHEET

CONFLICT SITUATION	WHAT I DO	HOW I FEEL
1. When someone blames me for something I didn't do…		
2. When someone puts me down or makes fun of me…		
3. When someone tells me to do something I don't want to do…		
4. When someone avoids me and appears to be angry or upset with me…		

VOWEL PLAY WORKSHEET (CONTINUED)

CONFLICT SITUATION	WHAT I DO	HOW I FEEL
5. When someone talks behind my back and says things that are lies…		
6. When someone tries to get me involved in a disagreement with others…		
7. When the teacher asks me to do something I know I can't do…		
8. When I am upset with a friend because he/she broke a promise…		
9. When I have a joint project that the other person won't seem to get involved with…		
10. Other		

OBJECTIVES:

1. Students will be able to identify five methods of responding to conflict.

2. Students will be able to distinguish the differing results when using each method.

3. Students will be able to appreciate the proper use of each method in responding to conflict.

SUPPLIES:

Chart paper

"Vowel Play" skits (reproducible provided)

PORTFOLIO ENTRY: *Life Roles,* Competency Skills, *"Relationship with Others"*

VOWEL PLAY CONTINUED
Life Roles
"Assertiveness Skills"

LESSON	NOTES

1. **Introduction:** Tell students that the lesson will review the five methods of responding to conflict. (Review the previous "Vowel Play" lesson.)

2. **Focus:** Ask students to think of conflict situations when they responded using one method and, in hindsight, know that another method would have been more successful.

3. **Activity:** Ask for volunteers to role play the skits. (See Vowel Play Skits.) After a brief private practice, have students perform them one skit at a time. After each response, label the response A,E,I,O,U and chart each on an escalator as to whether it escalated or de-escalated the conflict. Use **arrows to show** the rise or fall of the conflict. Discuss the responses and have students react to each response by the characters.

4. **Closure:** Ask: What did you learn from this lesson? What is the importance of this lesson? What did you learn about the escalation of conflict? Why is it important to use "I," "O," and "U" responses to conflict? Are "A" and "E" responses ever appropriate? Why?

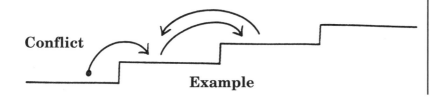

Conflict

Example

107

VOWEL PLAY SKITS

Jo and Ricki

Jo: (Bumps into Ricki.) Oops. Sorry.

Ricki: Watch where you're going.

Jo: Don't be so hyper!

Ricki: Buzz off!

Casey and Toni

Casey: We're never going to get this project done unless you start doing something on it.

Toni: It's not my fault if the library didn't have the books we needed. What was I supposed to do?

Casey: You're right. I'm just so nervous about this grade.

Toni: We've always done well in the past. Let's ask the teacher for some help.

Lee and Rae

Lee: Don't you know how to ask before you take something?

Rae: You said I could borrow your clothes as long as I return them clean and hung up.

Lee: Well, the deal is off.

Rae: I don't understand. What have I done to upset you?

VOWEL PLAY SKITS (CONTINUED)

Kyle and Desi

Kyle: Who left their stuff on my seat?

Desi: What's it to ya?

Kyle: I thought that maybe you needed it for your next class.

Desi: Yeah. I guess I probably do.

Jeri and Kim

Jeri: This group is going nowhere fast! We'll never get our project done.

Kim: We just need to organize ourselves better.

Jeri: Got any ideas?

Kim: Well, let's decide what needs to be done and how we should share the load.

Chris and Lauren

Chris: I am so mad at you. I thought you were going to call me.

Lauren: What are you talking about?

Chris: You know very well what I'm talking about!

Lauren: I can tell I've made you angry, but I honestly don't remember telling you I'd call. Remind me about our conversation.

OBJECTIVES:

1. Students will be able to recall times when they were treated inappropriately.

2. Students will learn skills to address problems of inappropriate treatment in the future.

3. Students will be able to practice these skills in a role play situation.

SUPPLIES:

Chart paper

Markers

PORTFOLIO ENTRY: *Life Roles,* Competency Skills, *"Relationship with Others"*

NO REGRETS

Life Roles

"Assertiveness Skills"

LESSON	NOTES
1. **Introduction:** Review the lesson entitled "I've Been a Tact."	

1. **Introduction:** Review the lesson entitled "I've Been a Tact."

2. **Focus:** Ask students to define the terms "tact" and "assertive." What is the difference? Which is more difficult to put into practice?

3. **Activity:** This activity has three parts:

   A. **Brainstorm:** Have students brainstorm experiences they have had when they have felt coerced into situations with adults and peers that have left them feeling powerless and full of regret. Chart the responses.

   B. **Refusal Skills:** Now ask them to suggest new ways to respond that would have made them feel better about the situation. Label this chart "Refusal Skills." Suggestions from the class should include: asking more questions, stating the problem, labeling the action as inappropriate or illegal, suggesting alternatives, refusing outright, arguing, expressing feelings tactfully, talking to someone else, and leaving the situation.

   C. **Role Play:** In groups of three, role play the brainstormed experiences using one or more of the refusal skills.

4. **Closure:** Ask: What did you learn about assertiveness? What will be the hardest factors to overcome in order to incorporate them into your life? When is assertiveness most difficult? What do you still need to work on to be more assertive?

5. **Follow–up:** "Write the Right" lesson on page 112.

111

WRITE AND RIGHT
Life Roles
"Assertiveness Skills"

OBJECTIVES:

1. Students will be able to recall times when they have been treated inappropriately.

2. Students will be able to appreciate the value of written assertiveness.

3. Students will be able to generate a tactful yet assertive written piece that addresses the situation.

SUPPLIES:

"Write and Right" follow-up worksheet

PORTFOLIO ENTRY: *Life Roles,* Competency Skills, *"Life Roles Affected by Others"*

WRITE THE RIGHT
Life Roles
"Assertiveness Skills"

LESSON	NOTES
1. **Introduction:** Review the "No Regrets" lesson previously covered.	
2. **Focus:** Ask students if there are alternative methods to addressing a wrongdoing. Suggestions might include: approaching a superior of the person, ignoring it, and addressing it in writing.	
3. **Activity:** Ask students for reasons that a situation might better be addressed in writing. These may include: an unsuccessful attempt in person, an inability to do it verbally, or feeling more comfortable addressing the situation in writing. Refer to the brainstormed list of experiences completed in the "No Regrets" lesson. Have students suggest which ones could have been handled better in writing or ask them for new suggestions. (A "letter to the editor" might be read as an example.) Assign students the writing of a tactful yet assertive letter that addresses an uncomfortable situation. Students should be encouraged to address real problems. Mailing the finished piece is optional.	
4. **Closure:** Ask: What did you learn about assertiveness? How can writing help you be assertive? Do you expect a response from your letter?	
5. **Follow-up:** Have students critique their letters using the follow-up worksheet.	

WRITE THE RIGHT FOLLOW-UP WORKSHEET

The letter being critiqued was written by _____.

The critic is _____.

1. Was the letter tactful? _____ Give examples of the use of tact.

   _____

   _____

   _____

2. Were feelings expressed appropriately? _____ Give examples.

   _____

   _____

   _____

3. Did grammar, spelling, etc. alter the effectiveness of the letter? _____
   How? Give examples.

   _____

   _____

   _____

4. How would you improve the letter? Give examples.

   _____

   _____

   _____

WRITE THE RIGHT FOLLOW–UP WORKSHEET

The letter being critiqued was written by **Kerry**_____.

The critic is **Terry**_____.

1. Was the letter tactful? _____**Yes**_____ Give examples of the use of tact.
   Said "I think you were wrong to act that way" instead of calling the person a name.
   _____
   _____

2. Were feelings expressed appropriately? _____**Yes**_____ Give examples.
   Used words like "frustrated" and "upset." I especially liked it when you said "It made my stomach churn
   for three days."
   _____

3. Did grammar, spelling, etc. alter the effectiveness of the letter? _____**Yes**_____
   How? Give examples.
   I found 5 misspelled words, and I think you put commas in the wrong place sometimes, like in the
   sentence where you describe what happened.
   _____

4. How would you improve the letter? Give examples.
   It would have been good if you could offer some suggestions for a better way of doing things.
   It will look better if you use a better font on your word processor. That one's hard to read.
   _____

GOOD BUY
Life Roles
"Use of Leisure Time"

OBJECTIVES:

1. Students will be able to choose and recreate popular television advertisements.

2. Students will be able to critique critical aspects of television advertising.

3. Students will be able to identify which aspects of television advertising influence their behaviors.

SUPPLIES:

Chart paper

Markers

"Good Buy" worksheet

PORTFOLIO ENTRY: *Life Roles, In My Spare Time, "Traits I Admire Most"*

GOOD BUY

Life Roles

"Use of Leisure Time"

LESSON	NOTES
1. **Introduction:** Tell students that today's lesson will address advertisements seen on television.	
2. **Focus:** Ask: How many TV ads do you see per day? Brainstorm a list of the most popular.	
3. **Activity:** Divide students into small groups and have them select one ad to recreate. (The teacher should know the choice of each group prior to rehearsing in order to provide a variety of samples and to approve the appropriateness of the skits. Keep props to a minimum.) Allow 10 minutes to prepare. Discuss each item on the worksheet, and add to it, if possible. After each group performs, have students individually fill out the worksheets, critiquing which factors most appealed to the viewers. Tally the results in a large group and discuss. Ask: Does the advertiser accurately represent the product? How have ads influenced your buying habits?	
4. **Closure:** Ask: What did you find most interesting about this lesson? Why did your group choose to recreate this ad? Which aspect of advertising influences you the most? How are ads geared to influencing us in our leisure time?	

GOOD BUY WORKSHEET

Name of Advertisement:

APPEAL FACTOR	BRIEF DESCRIPTION
Use of Humor	
Catchy Message	
Visual Effects	
Music/Lyrics	
Graphics	
Popular Spokesperson	
Entertaining	
New and Innovative	

GOOD BUY WORKSHEET

Name of Advertisement:
NIKE

APPEAL FACTOR	BRIEF DESCRIPTION
Use of Humor	**Very subtle, if any**
Catchy Message	**Just Do It!**
Visual Effects	**Great shots of athletes. Interesting angles and close-ups.**
Music/Lyrics	**Nothing outstanding. It doesn't block out the visual message.**
Graphics	**Simple, but VERY important. Just a check mark.**
Popular Spokesperson	**Michael Jordan, Tiger Woods, others.**
Entertaining	**Very entertaining. I look forward to the commercial.**
New and Innovative	**They change them often and they're always innovative.**

TIME CAPSULE
Life Roles
"Use of Leisure Time"

OBJECTIVES:

1. Students will be able to estimate the amount of time spent on daily activities.

2. Students will be able to survey their own use of time.

3. Students will be able to compare their estimates with factual data.

SUPPLIES:

"Time Capsule" worksheet

NOTE: This lesson has two parts that should be used four days apart.

PORTFOLIO ENTRY: *Life Roles, In My Spare Time, "Extracurricular"*

TIME CAPSULE
Life Roles
"Use of Leisure Time"

LESSON	NOTES
1. **Introduction:** Tell students that this will be a time-task analysis of their daily activities that will take three days.	
2. **Focus:** In small groups, have students come to consensus about the average amount of time spent by a teenager during a typical day on sleeping, eating, leisure, work, school, homework, chores, etc. Report out to large group and discuss. Assignment: Using the "Time Capsule" worksheet, keep track of the amount of time you spend doing daily activities for the next three days.	
3. **Activity:** Ask students to average the percentage of time spent doing each activity over the three-day period. Compare these averages to the small group consensus averages reached earlier and discuss.	
4. **Closure:** Ask: What did you learn from the comparison? What would you like to change? Does your use of time make you feel productive? How would others evaluate your use of time?	
5. **Follow–up:** Go to the Time Capsule Continued lesson that immediately follows.	

TIME CAPSULE WORKSHEET

Directions: In 15–minute intervals, report how you actually spend your time over a 3–day period.

Example:

	Day 1 (Thursday)	Day 2 (Friday)	Day 3 (Saturday)
11:00 a.m.	Eat—45/School—15	Eat—45/School—15	Sleep—15/Eat—15/ Leisure—30
12:00 p.m.	School—1 hr.	School—1 hr.	Leisure—1 hr.
1:00 p.m.	School—45/Leisure—15	School—45/Leisure—15	Rake yard—1 hr.

	Day #1	Day #2	Day #3
6:00 a.m.			
7:00			
8:00			
9:00			
10:00			
11:00			
12:00 p.m.			
1:00			
2:00			
3:00			
4:00			
5:00			
6:00			
7:00			
8:00			
9:00			
10:00			
11:00			

Name **Wayan** _____ Date _____

TIME CAPSULE WORKSHEET

Directions: In 15–minute intervals, report how you actually spend your time over a 3–day period.

Example:

	Day 1 (Thursday)	Day 2 (Friday)	Day 3 (Saturday)
11:00 a.m.	Eat—45/School—15	Eat—45/School—15	Sleep—15/Eat—15/Leisure—30
12:00 p.m.	School—1 hr.	School—1 hr.	Leisure—1 hr.
1:00 p.m.	School—45/Leisure—15	School—45/Leisure—15	Rake yard—1 hr.

	Day #1 Friday	Day #2 Saturday	Day #3 Sunday
6:00 a.m.	Sleep—15/Get ready—45	Sleep—1 hr.	Sleep—1 hr.
7:00	School—1 hr.	Sleep—1 hr.	Sleep—1 hr.
8:00	School—1 hr.	Sleep—1 hr.	Sleep—1 hr.
9:00	School—30/Leisure—30	Sleep—1 hr.	Get ready—30/Eat—30
10:00	Leisure—15/School—45	Sleep—30/Get ready—30	Travel—1 hr.
11:00	School—15/Lunch—45	Eat—30/TV—30	See grandparents—1 hr.
12:00 p.m.	School—1 hr.	Play ball—1 hr.	GP—1 hr.
1:00	School 45/Leisure—15	Play ball—1 hr.	GP—1 hr.
2:00	Sports—1 hr.	Shower—30/TV—30	Eat—1 hr.
3:00	Sports—1 hr.	TV—1 hr.	GP—1 hr.
4:00	Leisure—1 hr.	Phone—30/TV—30	Travel—1 hr.
5:00	Leisure—30/Dinner—30	Dinner—1 hr.	Phone—30/Leisure—30
6:00	Dishes—30/TV—30	Get Ready—1 hr.	TV—1 hr.
7:00	Homework—1 hr.	Friends—1 hr.	Dinner—30/TV—30
8:00	TV—1 hr.	Dance/School—1 hr.	Homework—1 hr.
9:00	Homework—1 hr.	Dance—1 hr.	Homework—1 hr.
10:00	Homework—30/Bed—30	Dance—1 hr.	Leisure—30/Sleep—30
11:00	Sleep→	Hang out 30/Home-TV/30	Sleep→

OBJECTIVES:

1. Students will be able to evaluate whether external factors are valid reasons for their use of personal time.

2. Students will be able to identify the difficulties in attempting to change behaviors.

3. Students will be able to commit to a personal action plan that alters behavior in one time category.

SUPPLIES:

Chart paper

Markers

"Time Capsule" worksheet (completed)

PORTFOLIO ENTRY: *Life Roles,* Balance

TIME CAPSULE CONTINUED
Life Roles
"Use of Leisure Time"

LESSON	NOTES
1. **Introduction:** Ask: Who comments on your use of time? (Examples may include parents, teachers, peers, employers, etc.) What do they say? What are your reactions?	
2. **Focus:** Ask: Looking back on your Time Capsule worksheet, do you agree with their comments on your use of time? What could you change?	
3. **Activity:** Brainstorm the difficulties in changing behavior related to time. (Examples: work schedule, long-term projects, unexpected happenings, etc.) Have students individually commit to changing one time category (e.g., eating, sleeping, leisure time, school work, etc.). Report daily on the progress to some member of the class.	
4. **Closure:** Ask: What difficulties were encountered? What personal discipline was needed to use your time productively? Were you successful in your plan? Why? Why not? Do you intend to continue your new behavior? How difficult will that be?	
5. **Follow-up:** Check the results after a period of time.	

CHAPTER SIX

Start Your Engines

Lessons to Promote Educational Development

Students can learn that their educational development is like tuning the engine of a car. If great care and attention has been put into both the design and the assembly of that engine, as well as its proper maintenance, then the vehicle should run smoothly. Students are also acutely aware that if they plan to have a driver's license, they need to complete an approved driver education course. Knowing the rules of the road helps one to be a safe driver. It's helpful if we learn some defensive driving skills, too.

A driver education course starts with the basics, and moves to the more advanced skills needed to responsibly handle a car. Even simple tasks like how to turn the key in the ignition, how to put the car in gear, how and when to step on the accelerator, and how to step on the brake are all given attention in the early sessions. Of course, lots of us knew how to do these things before the driver education class, but the course is designed to make sure everyone knows the basics. Students' educational development is no different. The relevance of one's education needs to be reinforced often, so that students see the relationship of their education to their success in life. The educational basics need to attend to readiness factors (turning the key in the ignition), classifying learning experiences (putting it in gear), finding sources of motivation (stepping on the accelerator), and recognizing limitations and challenges (stepping on the brakes).

Advanced drivers still need to continue learning as they mature. That's why automobile clubs send out magazines with tips for driving in hazardous weather, as well as research reports that enlighten us about safety issues, traffic statistics, and driving preferences. And when it comes to life's journeys, they also let us know about some great vacation opportunities!

Even race car drivers find it necessary to be well educated if they are to be successful. They use a combination of their knowledge and their experience to run a better race. They also learn from their mistakes. Racers and their pit crews always have a checklist of items to verify before a race to make sure every part is in working order. The concept of lifelong learning has many role models and metaphors.

In this chapter, the lessons and activities on educational development are designed to help students appreciate and invest in their educational opportunities as they seek career fulfillment. The five components of Educational Development that are addressed are: Thinking and Learning, Assessment Skills, Work Habits, Social and Economic Foundations, and Academic Planning. Educational development in the career decision-making process is like having smart drivers and cars with well-tuned engines. If everything is in working order, the engine should start the first time and keep running smoothly, with only occasional stops for refueling and minor maintenance.

OBJECTIVES:

1. Students will be able to list and define Gardner's seven intelligences.

2. Students will be able to categorize the intelligence strengths of well-known personalities and themselves.

3. Students will be able to generate lessons that incorporate each intelligence strength.

SUPPLIES:

"Gardner's Seven Intelligences" information sheet

"Pollution" worksheet

Optional Resource: Armstrong, T. *Multiple Intelligences in the Classroom,* Alexandria, VA: ASCD (1994).

PORTFOLIO ENTRY: *Educational Development,* Learning Style

Educational Development

"Thinking and Learning"

LESSON	NOTES

1. **Introduction:** Give an example of a time when you did not feel very intelligent. Ask students to give examples of situations when they did not feel intelligent. Have them describe the details of the situation.

2. **Focus:** Tell students that intelligence is not always knowing the right answer, but rather a broad scope of human capabilities that solve problems and create products in a natural setting. Present the information sheet and discuss the seven intelligences described.

3. **Activity:** Ask students to think of well-known personalities who may possess an intelligence strength (Examples: Thomas Jefferson—logical/mathematical, Ghandi—intrapersonal). Now ask students, in small groups, to discuss their individual intelligence strengths. Have them ask for classmates' input if necessary.

   Hand out the "Solutions to Pollution" worksheet. In small groups, ask students to create activities for each of the seven intelligences on the topic of "pollution." Give ample time for the groups to work and give support to their ideas for solutions to the pollution problem.

4. **Closure:** Ask: Why is it important to know this information? How does it change your ideas about "intelligence?" How can you use it to help you do better in school? Who should know about your intelligence strength?

GARDNER'S SEVEN INTELLIGENCES

 WORD SMART (linguistic intelligence)—the ability to use words and language (e.g., authors, speech writers, lawyers, politicians, journalists, sports analysts).

 NUMBER SMART (logical-mathematical intelligence)—the ability to use numbers and logic and see relationships (e.g., scientists, computer engineers, accountants, problem solvers, bankers).

 PICTURE SMART (spatial intelligence)—the ability to be sensitive to form, shape, color, and design (e.g., illustrators, photographers, cartoonists, interior designers, architects).

 BODY/SPORT/HAND SMART (bodily-kinesthetic intelligence)—the ability to use one's whole body to express ideas and feelings (e.g., film makers, dancers, athletes, martial artists, chiropractors, machinists).

 MUSIC SMART (musical intelligence)—the ability to enjoy rhythm and music and play instruments (e.g., rock stars, rappers, church organists, music therapists, choir members).

 PEOPLE SMART (interpersonal intelligence)—the ability to work successfully with people (e.g., talk show hosts, salespeople, educators, managers, receptionists).

 SELF SMART (intrapersonal intelligence)—the ability to work accurately by one's self and know one's strengths (e.g., entrepreneurs or "self-made" people, people who keep journals, people who meditate, philosophers).

SOLUTIONS TO POLLUTION WORKSHEET

Directions: Think of an activity for each topic which would allow each intelligence to express itself. Use additional space, if needed.

WORD SMART
_____
_____
_____

NUMBER SMART
_____
_____
_____

PICTURE SMART
_____
_____
_____

BODY SMART
_____
_____

MUSIC SMART
_____
_____
_____

PEOPLE SMART
_____
_____
_____

SELF SMART
_____
_____

LEARNING IN STYLE
Educational Development
"Thinking and Learning"

OBJECTIVES:

1. Students will be able to complete a learning styles inventory.

2. Students will be able to understand and interpret the results of the inventory.

3. Students will be able to explain their learning styles in a group presentation by demonstrating their learning styles.

NOTE: This lesson may take two class periods.

SUPPLIES:

Learning Styles Inventories (of your choice):

Barsch, J. *Barsch Learning Style Inventory.* Novato, CA: Academic Therapy.

Dunn, R. S., Dunn, K., and Price, G. E. *Learning Style Inventory.* Lawrence, KS: Price Systems.

McCarthy, B. *4MAT.* Barrington, IL: Excel.

Meisgeier, C. and Murphy, E. *Murphy-Meisgeier Type Indicator for Children.* Palo Alto, CA: Consulting Psychologists Press.

Oakland, T., Glutting, J. J., and Horton, C. B. *Student Styles Questionnaire.* San Antonio, TX: Psychological Corporation.

PORTFOLIO ENTRY: *Educational Development,* Learning Style or Learning Assets

LEARNING IN STYLE
Educational Development
"Thinking and Learning"

LESSON	NOTES
1. **Introduction:** Tell students that they will be taking a learning style inventory.	
2. **Focus:** Use published directions that come with the learning style inventory to explain the procedures for taking the assessment.	
3. **Activity:** When the inventory is scored, use the published information that comes with it to explain how the results are interpreted. Discuss in sufficient detail so students understand their scores. Divide the class into groups by their dominant learning style. Assign them the task of making a presentation that explains their learning style by *using* their learning style. Encourage creativity.	
4. **Closure:** Ask: What modifications can you make in your approach to learning that will take advantage of your learning style? How can this knowledge be applied to other areas of your life?	

BLOOMIN' SCHOLARS

Educational Development

"Thinking and Learning"

OBJECTIVES:

1. Students will be able to define Bloom's higher levels (taxonomy) of thinking and learning.

2. Students will be able to apply the levels to a given piece of written work.

3. Students will be able to apply the levels to academic subjects.

SUPPLIES:

"Bloom's Higher Levels of Learning" worksheet

Teacher-generated poem, song, prose, or short story

PORTFOLIO ENTRY: *Educational Development,* Thinking Skills or Learning Assets

BLOOMIN' SCHOLARS

Educational Development

"Thinking and Learning"

LESSON	NOTES
1. **Introduction:** Tell students that learning relies primarily on asking questions, receiving answers, and finding ways to use the information. The types of questions asked can elicit rote memory answers or answers that require higher levels of thinking.	
2. **Focus:** Tell students that you will be teaching them six levels of thinking developed by Benjamin Bloom. (See "Bloom's Higher Levels of Learning" handout.)	
3. **Activity:** Distribute handout. Discuss each level, starting with the lowest level (knowledge) and progressing to the higher levels. Explain that each level builds on the next. Using a written piece (e.g., a fable, a nursery rhyme, a song with a message, a story, or a poem), have small groups of students develop questions about the piece at each level. Have them share their questions with the entire class, and discuss the depth of thinking needed to answer the questions.	
4. **Closure:** Ask: Why is it important to know these levels of thinking? How can you apply this knowledge to your present academic subjects? How do higher-level thinking skills make you a better student? How can you use this information in the future? Why are higher-level thinking skills needed by workers in successful businesses?	

BLOOM'S HIGHER LEVELS OF LEARNING

Directions: Each of the levels of learning listed below requires different kinds of thinking and ways to use what we know. For each level, an explanation is given, followed by an example of how mathematics skills are used at the different levels. The "Questions asked" information provides you with some samples of the kinds of questions that are typically used to find out whether people can demonstrate their abilities at the various levels of learning.

Knowledge is considered the most "basic" level of learning. Start with the description and examples of KNOWLEDGE and then work your way up to the "higher" levels of learning. If you do not understand one of the levels, be sure to ask someone to explain it to you more clearly.

KNOWLEDGE

This level relies on rote memory and recall of facts. (Example: What is the answer to 4 − 1 = ? Answer: 3) Questions asked: What? Who? Where? When?

_____

_____

COMPREHENSION

This level requires understanding and explanation of information. (Example: Why is 543 − 100 = 433? A: In subtraction, the minuend is taken away from the subtrahend to give a remainder, or the amount that is still left.) Questions asked: Why? How? Can you explain?

_____

_____

APPLICATION

This level requires combining knowledge and comprehension to use in new situations. (Example: Chris started the week with a total of $402 in a savings account. On Monday, she withdrew $35 for concert tickets and on Friday withdrew $75 to pay for some work on her car. Does Chris still have enough money in her account to maintain the $300 minimum required to keep from having to pay a service charge?) Questions asked: How or in what way can this be applied?

_____

_____

BLOOM'S HIGHER LEVELS OF LEARNING (CONTINUED)

ANALYSIS

This level requires the separation of a coherent whole into diverse parts because you understand how those parts apply to a problem. (Example: You sit down to do your taxes for the first time. In looking over the columns and tables, what mathematical applications will you have to use?)

_____

_____

SYNTHESIS

This level requires the combination of diverse parts to create a coherent whole. (Example: Interview workers in the community and find occupations that require knowledge of all four basic mathematical functions on a regular basis. What are the implications of your findings?)

_____

_____

EVALUATION

This level requires determining something's worth or value based on rational application of all levels of learning. (Example: Should all students be required to demonstrate competence in mathematics? Why or why not?)

_____

_____

GETTING TESTY
Educational Development
"Assessment Skills"

OBJECTIVES:

1. Students will be able to reduce test anxiety by pre-test exploration and exercises.

2. Students will be able to view testing situations in a positive, controlled manner.

3. Students will be able to apply testing-taking strategies to other stressful situations.

SUPPLIES:

"Getting Testy Strategies" information sheet

"My Getting Testy Strategies" worksheet

PORTFOLIO ENTRY: *Educational Development,* Special Needs, Competency Skills, *"Attitudes Toward Learning"*

GETTING TESTY
Educational Development
"Assessment Skills"

LESSON	NOTES
1. **Introduction:** Tell students that this lesson and the following two lessons will be about tests and test taking.	
2. **Focus:** Ask how many students drive a car, can pilot a plane, will become an electrician, etc. (or any other profession that requires a test to determine competence). Tell them that all require tests. Ask: How do you feel before, during, and after tests?	
3. **Activity:** Tell students that they are going to discuss two necessary approaches to preparing themselves for testing situations. One approach is to review the information that will be covered on the test; the other is to prepare your attitude. When you do both, you become a ready tester. Teachers usually tell students the content covered by tests. But it is also important to prepare the test taker's attitude. Pass out the "Getting Testy Strategies" information sheets. Discuss the benefits of each strategy. Then pass out and have students complete their own worksheets.	
4. **Closure:** Ask: What did you learn about test taking? Why is it important? When and how could you apply these rules to other situations?	

GETTING TESTY STRATEGIES

The following strategies are often helpful for improving your performance on tests:

1. GET LOTS OF REST

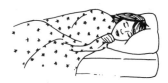

Get plenty of rest the night before a test. In fact, you will feel more rested if you have had several good nights of sleep before a test. Remember, too, that sometimes the foods you eat will affect how well you sleep.

2. ARREST THE STRESS

Try to reduce your level of stress by taking several deep breaths, relaxing your muscles, and briefly thinking about a pleasant thought. Resume taking the test after you have relaxed enough to stay focused and feel able to sort out the answers.

3. SAY YOU'RE THE BEST

Positive self-talk is the act of making positive comments to yourself over and over again until you really start believing the message. For example, you could say, "I've studied hard and I know this stuff," to remind yourself that you are prepared to pass this test. (Of course, you can only make such a statement if it's true!) Difficult questions and complex problem-solving tasks provide great opportunities to put self-talk tactics to work.

4. CLEAN UP THE MESS

Time management skills can help you more efficiently prepare for and take a test. If you are rather "scattered" in the way you typically do things, you should learn some time management skills to (a) help you organize your study time, and (b) wisely use the time to complete each section of a test and then recheck your answers.

MY GETTING TESTY STRATEGIES

Directions: List some specific strategies on this worksheet that you will use to try to improve your test-taking performance.

1. GET LOTS OF REST

_____

_____

_____

2. ARREST THE STRESS

_____

_____

_____

3. SAY YOU'RE THE BEST (What are your self-talk messages?)

_____

_____

_____

4. CLEAN UP THE MESS

_____

_____

_____

5. OTHER:

_____

_____

_____

OBJECTIVES:

1. Students will be able to define and discuss the term "competency."

2. Students will be able to choose an area in which to prove their competence.

3. Students will be able to prove their competency in one or more areas.

SUPPLIES:

Dictionary (optional)

PORTFOLIO ENTRY: *Educational Development,* Competency Skills, *"Relationship between Education and Career"*

PROVE IT!
Educational Development
"Assessment Skills"

LESSON	NOTES
1. **Introduction:** Ask students to define the term "competency." Use a dictionary if necessary.	
2. **Focus:** Tell students that the trend today in education, the arts, the sciences, the trades, the helping professions, etc. is competency-based assessment. Discuss.	
3. **Activity:** Ask students to brainstorm areas in which they feel they have a certain amount of competence. Examples may include: child care, mechanics, crafts, woodworking, piano, waiting/bussing tables, snow plowing, camp counselor, cooking, etc. Ask each student to choose one area and "prove" his/her competence. Students should be encouraged to choose an area that might be useful when seeking employment or admittance to post-secondary institutions. Competency-based proof might include: a list of skills, letters of recommendation, a product, a performance, a portfolio, etc. Share reports in small or large groups.	
4. **Closure:** Ask: Is competency-based assessment a fair method to evaluate a person's skills? Was this a difficult assignment? Can you give an example of a better method of assessment?	
5. **Follow-up:** Have students from other groups or classes evaluate/critique students' evidence of competence.	

THIS IS A TEST, BEEEP!

Educational Development

"Assessment Skills"

OBJECTIVES:

1. Students will be able to understand what a specific assessment tool is measuring.

2. Students will be able to generate questions that will help them explore the meaning of test results.

3. Students will be able to demonstrate how they can use assessment tools in making life decisions.

SUPPLIES:

Published assessments (examples: achievement tests, aptitude tests, interest inventories, personality assessments, placement tests, learning styles inventories)

PORTFOLIO ENTRY: *Educational Development,* Achievement

THIS IS A TEST, BEEEP!
Educational Development
"Assessment Skills"

LESSON	NOTES
1. **Introduction:** Tell students that assessment tools provide important information that can be used in decision making. Discuss their personal perceptions of these tools.	
2. **Focus:** Introduce one or more instruments that are used by the school to aid in student assessment (for example, achievement tests, interest inventories, college admissions tests, etc.). Provide students with an overview of what the assessment tool is measuring. Ask: What does this mean to you as a learner? How is it important? Have students compare and contrast their perceptions with the literature.	
3. **Activity:** Individually, have students rank themselves in each area of the assessment measures as low, medium, high (even though they may not have received the actual assessment results). In small groups, have students brainstorm how they might use their personal scoring information in various decision-making situations (e.g., course selection, career choice, post-secondary training programs, improvement of study habits, relationship issues).	
4. **Closure:** Ask: How can assessment information be helpful in a learning situation? When is it not helpful? How have your perceptions of assessment tools changed?	
5. **Follow-up:** Have students enter results in "Get a Life" or a personal portfolio. Provide interested students with their assessment results. Identify other assessment instruments that would help students with their decision making.	

145

NO LOBSTERS
Educational Development
"Work Habits"

OBJECTIVES:

1. Students will be able to brainstorm a list of learning and study skills that are necessary to be a successful student.

2. Students will be able to verbalize the problems that they have with each skill.

3. Students will be able to decide whether improvement in the skills can be accomplished by personal effort or with the help of the teacher.

SUPPLIES:

Chart paper

Four different color markers

"NO LOBSTERS" worksheet

NO LOBSTERS

Educational Development

"Work Habits"

LESSON	NOTES
1. **Introduction:** Tell students that this lesson will investigate some learning skills that they may already have developed to some degree, and could possibly improve.	
2. **Focus:** On a chart or chalkboard, write the letters of the words NO LOBSTERS vertically. Each letter stands for a learning skill that is necessary to develop to become a successful student. Have students suggest (guess) what the skills are. As students guess correctly, fill in the answer next to the letter (Note taking, Organization, Listening, Observation, Behavior, Studying, Time management, Exam taking, Reference skills, Style of learning). Discuss each.	
3. **Activity:** Form three evenly-spaced vertical columns after the list of skills. Label each, in different colors—PROBLEMS, STUDENT SOLUTIONS, TEACHER SOLUTIONS. Also pass out "NO LOBSTERS" worksheet, to students. Have students identify and chart in small or large groups the problems they have applying each skill, what action students could take to improve the skill, and what a teacher could do to increase the success of the skill.	
4. **Closure:** Ask: What did you learn from this lesson? How could these suggestions improve your study habits?	
5. **Follow-up:** Ask students to prepare for the next lesson by sharing the three skills they find most difficult to master and one goal that they could set to improve the skill. Continue with "NO LOBSTERS—II."	

NO LOBSTERS

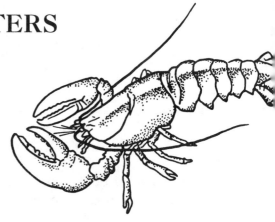

		PROBLEMS	STUDENT SOLUTIONS	TEACHER SOLUTIONS
N	Note Taking			
O	Organization			
L	Listening			
O	Observation			
B	Behavior			
S	Studying			
T	Time Management			
E	Exam Taking			
R	Reference Skills			
S	Style of Learning			

Sample student worksheet

NO LOBSTERS

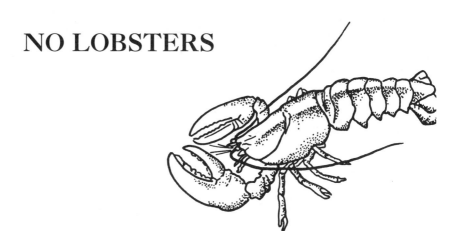

		PROBLEMS	STUDENT SOLUTIONS	TEACHER SOLUTIONS
N	Note Taking	sometimes don't write down the important stuff	study group— improve notes	Tell us when we should write something in our notes
O	Organization	Wait until the last minute.	Create a schedule; keep a calendar or assignment notebook	Require assignment notebook
L	Listening	Daydream	Pay attention	Sit daydreamers closer to front of room
O	Observation	Only observe if it's interesting	Stand up to see see things better	Make things more fun to observe
B	Behavior	Sometimes kid around too much.	Decide when it's ok to be funny	Just tell us when to get serious
S	Studying	Don't like to do homework.	Find a place and time to study	Reward for completing homework
T	Time Management	Do my homework when I'm too tired	start homework by 7:00	Goal sheets in school.
E	Exam Taking	Do a lot of cramming	Find person to study with	Do exam reviews
R	Reference Skills	Lazy about looking things up.	Keep reference books near study place	Do a lesson on reference skills
S	Style of Learning	Not sure what my learning style is.	Try to figure it out.	Give learning styles assessment.

NO LOBSTERS—II
Educational Development
"Work Habits"

OBJECTIVES:

1. Students will become able to be familiar with basic learning skills, problems in developing them, and possible solutions.

2. Students will be able to set at least three goals to improve their learning skills.

3. Students will be able to evaluate which skills would apply to the world of work.

SUPPLIES:

"NO LOBSTERS" worksheet (from previous lesson)

Markers

NO LOBSTERS—II
Educational Development
"Work Habits"

LESSON	NOTES
1. **Introduction:** Ask students to recall the NO LOBSTERS lesson. See if students can list the skills without looking at the chart.	
2. **Focus:** Ask students to individually identify the skill they find to be the most difficult to develop. Group students according to their selection. (Example: All students whose first choice is time management would be in the same group.)	
3. **Activity:** Tell groups they have 10 minutes to examine why the skill is so difficult for them and set at least three goals that group members could set to improve the skill. Have each group select a person to report to the large group. Share the in-depth problems and goals. Ask each student in the class to make a written commitment to no more than three goals suggested by the class. Ask for a report of their progress during the week.	
4. **Closure:** Ask: What was the purpose of this lesson? When have learning skills been discussed before? Who should be responsible to teach students learning skills? Can you remember when you learned any of them? Which skills would be important to have in a job? Are some skills more necessary in certain jobs? Give examples.	
5. **Follow-up:** This lesson can be reviewed periodically throughout the school year. Charts can be devised to show the progress students are making by improved grades or teacher commendations.	

LEARN 'N EARN
Educational Development
"Work Habits"

OBJECTIVES:

1. Students will be able to be familiar with their basic study skills and the problems they encounter in learning.

2. Students will be able to recognize how study skills apply to the workplace.

3. Students will be able to apply this knowledge in a work-related role play.

SUPPLIES:

"Learn 'n Earn" role play sheets

NOTE: Role Play Sheet #1 is easier; Role Play Sheet #2 is more difficult.

PORTFOLIO ENTRY: *Educational Development,* Competency Skills, *"Relationship between Education and Career"*

LEARN 'N EARN
Educational Development
"Work Habits"

LESSON	NOTES
1. **Introduction:** Tell students that school is a preparation for their life work.	
2. **Focus:** Brainstorm work habits that are necessary to succeed in school and to handle the problems students encounter in learning. Ask them to explore how these same skills would be applied to a work situation.	
3. **Activity:** Hand out role play sheets. Have students form pairs and carry out role play situations (See "Role Play" sheets.)	
4. **Closure:** For Interviewee: Ask: How difficult was it to link study skills and work habits to a work situation?	

4. **Closure:** For Interviewee: Ask: How difficult was it to link study skills and work habits to a work situation?

For Employer: Ask: How can you evaluate the potential success of the candidate based on the examples given in the interview?

For all: Ask: How difficult was this role play? Why was it important?

LEARN 'N EARN
ROLE PLAY SHEET #1

Props: 2 chairs, a desk or table

Scenario: The employer meets with an employee to provide feedback from a Job Performance Review that was completed after the first six months on the job. The employer cites some "areas of deficiency" that have been a concern (e.g., late for work, long breaks, errors in work reports). The employee is asked to suggest ways to improve the job performance evaluation.

Tasks:
1. Decide on the setting (perhaps a local business) and a specific job title for the employee.

2. Employer: Set a positive but firm tone for the role; do not play extreme roles, such as a tyrant boss or one who "lets anything go."

3. Employee: Try to be as specific as possible in describing new work habits you will bring to the job in the next six months.

LEARN 'N EARN
ROLE PLAY SHEET #2

Props: 2 chairs, a desk or table

Scenario: The employer meets with a new employee to discuss an important project the company will be initiating in the next few weeks. The project will require that several employees work for quite a while to create individual parts of the project. Then they will all regroup as a project team to create a system that links all the parts. From there, the team will decide how to involve others in the company on this project. The employer needs to be convinced that this employee can work both independently and as part of a project team.

Tasks: 1. Decide on the setting and the job titles for each role player.

2. Employer: Set the tone for the meeting (i.e., act businesslike). Think about what kind of information you will need to help you decide if the employee should be put on the project.

3. Employee: Use examples to illustrate the kinds of study skills or work habits that qualify you to be a member of the team.

BECOMING A PRO
Educational Development
"Work Habits"

OBJECTIVES:

1. Students will be able to understand the concept of professional development and interview a worker about it.

2. Students will be able to draw conclusions from the collected interview data on professional development.

3. Students will be able to explore how current skills relate to future practices on the job.

SUPPLIES:

"Becoming a Pro" interview sheet

BECOMING A PRO
Educational Development
"Work Habits"

LESSON	NOTES

1. **Introduction:** Tell students that the lesson will explore how employees use and develop study skills and work habits on the job.

2. **Focus:** Introduce the concept of professional development by asking students to brainstorm examples (e.g., OJT, workshops, training courses, licensing exams, apprenticeship programs, management training, etc.). How do such programs enhance the performance of employees and the success of the company?

3. **Activity:** In preparation for an interview with an employed worker, brainstorm who might be a potential candidate for an interview. Encourage students to find positive role models to interview. Give the assignment to interview an employee, using the "Becoming a Pro" interview sheet. Set a completion date.

4. **Activity continued:** In small groups, share the interview information. Have students draw conclusions from the collective data (Examples: professional development—not valued/strongly encouraged; independently sought/provided; voluntary/mandatory).

5. **Closure:** Ask: What have you learned from the interview? How will your present personal study skills and work habits contribute to your future professional development?

BECOMING A PRO INTERVIEW SHEET

Name: _____ Position: _____

Company: _____

What are your major job responsibilities?

_____
_____
_____
_____
_____

What skills and knowledge were necessary for you to acquire after taking this position?

_____
_____
_____
_____
_____

How did you acquire these skills?

_____
_____
_____
_____
_____

BECOMING A PRO INTERVIEW SHEET
(CONTINUED)

How do you prefer to learn new skills and knowledge?

_____

_____

_____

_____

_____

How important is professional development to this company?

_____

_____

_____

_____

_____

What are your future professional development plans?

_____

_____

_____

_____

_____

OBJECTIVES:

1. Students will be able to choose a local controversial issue that has social and economic ramifications.

2. Students will be able to investigate the pros and cons of each side.

3. Students will be able to draw conclusions about the social and economic consequences of each side.

SUPPLIES:

Newspapers

Town reports

Guest speakers

PROS AND CONS

Educational Development

"Social and Economic Development"

LESSON	NOTES
1. **Introduction:** Tell students that this lesson will be discussed during a number of classes and will deal with local issues that will affect them in the future.	
2. **Focus:** Ask students to read the local paper for the next week and keep track of the local issues that will have social and economic ramifications for them and their families.	
3. **Activity:** Ask students to list the major controversial local issues. In small groups, have students decide on one issue that is interesting to them and is researchable. Have students choose sides and develop points for debate. Ask them to focus on the effects on the people and the cost to the community. Provide them with minutes of community meetings, available documents, and guest speakers, if possible, or have them interview community leaders. Have each side give its arguments in a 10-minute presentation to a neutral, unbiased class or group. (Encourage visual displays.) Have observers determine the stronger arguments and give their reasons why.	
4. **Closure:** Ask: What did you learn from this lesson? Why are social and economic issues so controversial? What do you predict the real outcome will be? Why is it important to keep abreast of these issues? How can skills and knowledge learned in school be used to help people decide controversial issues?	
5. **Follow-up:** Have individuals write about their class debate or discuss it with involved community members.	

OBJECTIVES:

1. Students will be able to investigate a social need that will influence the local/state economy.

2. Students will be able to develop questions and express concerns about the social need to a knowledgeable community resource person.

3. Students will be able to process the information and draw conclusions from the speaker's presentation.

SUPPLIES:

Community speaker

"What's the Price?" Reference Information Sheet

Sample Letter of Appreciation

NOTE: This lesson will take 2 to 3 class periods.

PORTFOLIO ENTRY: *Educational Development,* Competency Skills, *"Societal Needs"*

WHAT'S THE PRICE?

Educational Development

"Social and Economic Foundations"

LESSON	NOTES
1. **Introduction:** Ask students to brainstorm social needs that would have an impact on the economy. Examples may include: aid to education, job training for the unemployed, increased welfare aid, increased police services, increased number of social service workers.	
2. **Focus:** Ask students to come to consensus on one topic to investigate.	
3. **Activity:** Allow students time to research the issue, and develop a list of speakers who could appropriately address the issue. Ask them to develop questions and a list of concerns that a speaker could address. Have a small group write a letter of invitation to a potential guest speaker, including their issues. In anticipation of the appearance of the speaker, set guidelines for student behavior, especially if the issue is controversial. Carry out guest speaker presentation.	
4. **Closure:** After the presentation, ask: Was a balanced viewpoint presented? What did you learn from this experience? How would you vote on this issue? Will this social issue benefit you? What effect will it have on you financially? Will it affect your parents?	
5. **Follow-up:** Ask for a volunteer to write a letter of appreciation to the speaker. Include in the letter the effect the exploration of the issue had on the class and the class' consensus on the issue.	

WHAT'S THE PRICE?
REFERENCE INFORMATION FOR INSTRUCTOR

I. **POSSIBLE TOPICS (social needs that have an impact on the economy):**

- Welfare fraud
- Pollution
- Lack of recreational facilities for youth
- Loitering
- Racism
- Sexism
- Ageism
- Illegal aliens
- Gangs

II. **SAMPLE QUESTIONS TO ASK SPEAKERS**

- How does (issue) affect people who work in various jobs?
- Could you give some examples of how this issue has been a problem in our area?
- What legal rights do people have to fight these problems?
- Are there any positive effects on the economy because of this issue?
- What can students do to address the problem?

SAMPLE LETTER OF APPRECIATION

Date

Heading
(name & title)
(street address)
(city, state, zip)

Dear _____:

We would like to thank you for visiting our social studies class on (date) to discuss how the issue of (type of issue) has many influences on our economy. We thought it was important to see both the problems and the ways jobs are created as a result of the problems.

As we discussed your presentation in class, we all agreed that the example you gave about the case in the (name) neighborhood really made us understand how difficult the problem is. Thank you for sharing your experience and interest in the topic. We will all be more aware of our responsibility for doing something about (issue) in the future.

Sincerely,

The American Studies Class at
Amerigo Vespucci High School

OBJECTIVES:

1. Students will be able to create an interview survey for community members to answer.

2. Students will be able to successfully interview the community members.

3. Students will be able to draw conclusions about the value of education as it relates to the community.

SUPPLIES:

List of community members

News articles on social/economic issues

PORTFOLIO ENTRY: *Educational Development,* Competency Skills, *"Societial Needs"*

BUILDING A FOUNDATION
Educational Development
"Social and Economic Foundations"

LESSON	NOTES
1. **Introduction:** Ask students to discuss the value of an educated community as it relates to social and economic issues. (Examples may be given from local newspapers to stimulate discussion.)	
2. **Focus:** Tell students that they will be creating an interview questionnaire and doing interviews of local community members on this topic. Based on the preceding discussion, have students brainstorm what questions might be asked to elicit the information they wish to gain.	
3. **Activity:** When numerous questions are brainstormed, combine and eliminate until there are approximately eight questions that are clear and concise. (Two sample questions are: 1. Do you consider an educated community important when making social and financial decisions? Why? 2. If you had the opportunity to continue your education, would you, and why?)	
4. **Closure:** In small groups, have students draw conclusions from their interviews. Share in the larger group and consolidate the results.	
5. **Follow-up:** Publish the results of the questionnaire and submit them to the school or local newspaper. Write thank-you letters to contributors and inform them of the results.	

IT'S A PLAN
Educational Development
"Academic Planning"

OBJECTIVES:

1. Students will become aware of future educational choices and options.

2. Students will be able to make tentative secondary-school course choices.

3. Students will be able to defend their choices based on their past academic histories and future career interests.

SUPPLIES:

Secondary handbooks for the middle schools or high schools in your school district. The handbooks should give course titles and descriptions, as well as information about special programs.

Course/program options available in the school counselors' office or the main office.

PORTFOLIO ENTRY: *Educational Development,* Competency Skills, *"Educational and Career Decisions"*

IT'S A PLAN

Educational Development

"Academic Planning"

LESSON	NOTES
1. **Introduction:** Tell students that they are going to be given the opportunity to plan for the future.	
2. **Focus:** Pass out secondary-school handbooks and course/program options. Allow students time to read the material. Discuss the format of the handbook and answer questions pertaining to a secondary-school diploma and your state requirements.	
3. **Activity:** Allow students to work in pairs or small groups to make a tentative four-year academic plan. Encourage students to keep their past academic successes and career interests in mind. When completed, have students defend their choices to a partner.	
4. **Closure:** Ask: Why did we do this lesson? What did you learn from this experience? What was most interesting to you? What was difficult? What options were you unaware of?	
5. **Follow-up:** Have high school counselors visit with the class and answer any questions about registration, requirements, prerequisites, etc. Investigate the options available in private or special-interest secondary schools.	

OBJECTIVES:

1. Students will be able to draw conclusions from a sample of portfolio entries.

2. Students will be able to complete a portfolio entry entitled, "Things I Need to Know about My Own Learning."

3. Students will be able to draw conclusions from their own portfolio entries.

SUPPLIES:

"Eye Conclude" worksheet—Portfolio Model

"Eye Conclude" worksheet—Student Sample

PORTFOLIO ENTRY: *Educational Development,* Academic Planning, *Things I Need to Know*

EYE CONCLUDE...
Educational Development
"Academic Planning"

LESSON	NOTES

1. **Introduction:** Tell students that they will be researching their own future plans by investigating their successes in an academic setting.

2. **Focus:** Students will be given a model to investigate, and then will be given the task of completing the same kind of reflective response for themselves.

3. **Activity:** Present the mock portfolio entries of the "Eye Conclude" worksheet. Ask students to draw conclusions from the entries based on the general topic headings of the section (Examples: learning style; work habits; etc.).

   Assign students the task of filling in a blank portfolio worksheet and give ample time for thoughtful consideration of each section. Provide assistance for students who may have difficulty filling out the worksheet. In pairs or small groups, ask them to draw conclusions about their own entries.

4. **Closure:** Ask: What did you learn about drawing conclusions about others? How difficult or easy was it to make entries into the portfolio worksheet? What additional information would have been helpful? How did talking with others about your own entry make it possible to improve the final statements you included in your portfolio worksheet? What purpose will this portfolio entry serve in making your future academic plans?

5. **Follow-up:** The next lesson, "Window Shopping."

171

EYE CONCLUDE WORKSHEET
Things I Need to Know about My Own Learning

No test or assessment can be totally accurate in describing your unique abilities and achievement. However, both standardized tests and informal assessments can provide you with some very useful information as you discover more about your educational needs and talents.

LEARNING STYLE:

I have taken a Learning Style assessment and I have discussed the results. My primary Learning Style is:

ACHIEVEMENT:

What I've learned from the achievement tests I have taken:

LEARNING ASSETS:

Some of my learning strengths are (e.g., memory for details, how to analyze, memory tricks, problem solving):

SCHOOL WORK

Subjects in which I do well:

Subjects in which I have difficulty:

SPECIAL NEEDS:

The school helps some students identify special learning needs (if applicable). I need special help with:

WORK HABITS:

I have learned that my school work habits can best be described as:

THINKING SKILLS:

Some things I have learned about Thinking Skills (e.g., creativity, reasoning, "seeing with the mind's eye"):

EYE CONCLUDE WORKSHEET
Things I Need to Know about My Own Learning

No test or assessment can be totally accurate in describing your unique abilities and achievement. However, both standardized tests and informal assessments can provide you with some very useful information as you discover more about your educational needs and talents.

LEARNING STYLE:

I have taken a Learning Style assessment and I have discussed the results. My primary Learning Style is:

I need to see what I am learning but it helps even more if I can talk about it and see if I understand it. Visual diagrams help a lot. I hear everything around me, so I sometimes have to find a quiet room or plug my ears to concentrate.

ACHIEVEMENT:

What I've learned from the achievement tests I have taken:

I'm pretty good in math. I have really high scores in science too. My speeling scores were belowe average. Sometimes I have to read things twice before I catch on.

LEARNING ASSETS:

Some of my learning strengths are (e.g., memory for details, how to analyze, memory tricks, problem solving):

I pretty much confirmes what I already no: that I'm pretty good in sciences. My advissor says it means I have the "potential" to be good in sciences, but I alreedy no that. My only major weekness is in spelling and reading.

SCHOOL WORK

Subjects in which I do well:
Biology   Chemistry   Physical Education

Subjects in which I have difficulty:
Reading   Foreign Language   Spelling

SPECIAL NEEDS:

The school helps some students identify special learning needs (if applicable). I need special help with:

I get help 2 times a week with spelling and reading.

WORK HABITS:

I have learned that my school work habits can best be described as:

I like to work with my hands and figure out what is going on. I like to think about life and how it works.

THINKING SKILLS:

Some things I have learned about Thinking Skills (e.g., creativity, reasoning, "seeing with the mind's eye"):

Others do much better than me in reading, but I'm a good problem solver.

WINDOW SHOPPING
Educational Development
"Academic Planning"

OBJECTIVES:

1. Students will be able to identify and assess post-secondary training and educational opportunities that are of personal interest to them.

2. Students will be able to research post-secondary training and educational options using available resources.

3. Students will be able to match their past academic successes and strengths with viable future educational options.

SUPPLIES:

None

PORTFOLIO ENTRY: *Educational Development,* Academic Planning, *Plans after High School*

WINDOW SHOPPING
Educational Development
"Academic Planning"

LESSON	NOTES
1. **Introduction:** Ask the class to identify at least five possible career options they are considering after secondary school is completed. Share and chart these ideas, grouping them into three categories: working with things, working with people, and working with ideas.	
2. **Focus:** Ask students: What are the implications for future training and education if you are to enter these careers?	
3. **Activity:** Tell students that you will be introducing them to the resources available to research their educational and training options. (This may include: college handbooks, computer searches, talking to college and military representatives and/or college students, on-the-job training, apprenticeship programs, and available library resources, such as video tapes and flyers.) Have students brainstorm and agree upon factors to be considered (e.g., length of training, cost, location, competitive admissions, licensing, post-graduate job placement service.) Give students ample time to thoroughly absorb and process the material. (This may take a number of classes.)	
4. **Closure:** Ask: Which resource did you find most useful? Did you arrive at any decisions? What helped most in making those decisions?	
5. **Follow-up:** Assist students with applications, interviews, additional resource material, etc.	

CHAPTER SEVEN

The Roadmap

Lessons to Foster Career Exploration and Planning

If you know where you're starting and you know your destination, then the roadmap targets all the trails that need to be taken to get you where you want to go. One's career requires a road atlas. The traveler needs to have a global view of what's ahead, but also needs to know how many separate but interconnecting trips might also be required to really "see the world" in perspective and make it a truly rewarding journey.

Career decisions are not little day trips, although some day trips (like job shadowing) can provide major insights about what to avoid in the future and what you want to be sure to include in future trips. There are no simple roadmaps that illustrate the path to career success. However, students often need some of the small, simple maps that they can later compile into the atlases that will define their career journeys.

Of course, we know that some people choose to take adventurous routes in life. Such routes can be challenging and exciting, but they can also be unsettling or even disastrous if the proper precautions are not taken. Some people are more adaptable and resourceful in dealing with unforeseen emergencies along the way. In most cases, however, especially with major trips, people feel more confident when the trip is laid out before them. Students need good "map skills" to maneuver the career paths that lie before them.

A roadmap provides the traveler with the most direct route. Many even choose to call ahead to see if there is any road construction that will require extra time or rerouting. Students who deliberately plan their career paths feel more confident about where they are headed in life. They have investigated the prospects for success and have charted a course that complements their goals, their budgets, and their itineraries. The best planners have even considered alternative routes to their destination.

In this chapter, lesson plans are provided to address five different components of Career Exploration and Planning: The Career Planning Process, Using Career Information, Positive Work Attitudes, Career Decisions, and Job-Seeking Skills. The three lessons for each component provide a variety of opportunities for students to understand both the complexity of career planning and the specific skills needed to be successful in the world of work. This final set of lessons will also provide a framework for students to use in integrating some of the other lessons from previous chapters.

MAJOR MAJOR
Career Exploration and Planning
"Career Planning Process"

OBJECTIVES:

1. Students will be able to define a career major.

2. Students will be able to group career options into career major groups.

3. Students will be able to give reasons for the career major groupings.

SUPPLIES:

"Career Options" worksheet

Scissors

Glue or tape

PORTFOLIO ENTRY: *Career Exploration and Planning,* Competency Skills, *"Interpret Career Information"*

MAJOR MAJOR

Career Exploration and Planning

"Career Planning Process"

LESSON	NOTES
1. **Introduction:** Tell students that they will be identifying and working with the concept of a "career major."	
2. **Focus:** Define "career major" as a sequence of courses or a field of study that prepares a student for employment in a broad occupational or industrial cluster.	
3. **Activity:** In pairs, ask students to complete the worksheet, clustering similar career majors in boxes. Discuss. Students' answers may differ depending on their rationale for placement.	
4. **Closure:** Ask: What did you learn from this lesson? How did your worksheets compare with your classmates'? What does this exercise tell you about career planning?	
5. **Follow-up:** Have students ask parents to complete the worksheet. Have students compare theirs with those of their parents.	

CAREER OPTIONS WORKSHEET

Directions: Cut on dotted lines and have students group similar career majors in the boxes provided. Glue or tape your selections. Additional boxes may be added if necessary.

teacher

construction worker

librarian

crossing guard

factory worker

painter

car salesperson

nurse

foodserver

cashier

police officer

carpenter

lab technician

landscaper

electrician

lawyer

soldier

firefighter

ambulance driver

accountant

computer programmer

insurance agent

doctor

garbage collector

beautician

cartoonist

Possible Answers to
CAREER OPTIONS WORKSHEET

Students' answers may differ when they cluster career choices into the worksheet boxes. Their reasons for placement are important and should be discussed.

teacher
librarian
crossing guard

construction worker
factory worker
carpenter

nurse
doctor
ambulance driver
firefighter

painter
cartoonist

OBJECTIVES:

1. Students will be able to define the three stages of the career planning process.

2. Students will be able to critique their Personal Career Plans.

3. Students will be able to complete related entries in the portfolio.

SUPPLIES:

"Tentative Career Plan" worksheet

"Critiquing Your Responses" worksheet (only for users of the *Get a Life* portfolio)

PORTFOLIO ENTRY: *Career Exploration and Planning,* Competency Skills, *"Planning Process"*

PLAN-IT OF THE "AEPs"

Career Exploration and Planning

"Career Planning Process"

LESSON	NOTES
1. **Introduction:** Tell students that this lesson will review the career planning stages, and help them critique their tentative career plans and focus on more definite plans.	
2. **Focus:** Define and review the three career planning stages.	
3. **Activity:** Ask students to fill in the "Tentative Career Plan" worksheet. Have student partners help each other fill in the worksheets. If you are using the *Get a Life* portfolio, have students read and discuss the various sections of "My Personal Career Plan." Have students verbally share their responses to the critiquing questions in the Career Plan. After using these activities as a means of "reflective learning," have students fill in their portfolio Career Plans, demonstrating the "best work" related to Career Planning.	
4. **Closure:** Ask: How "close" is your career decision? How does this lesson help you in your career decisions? What are your next steps? How do you plan to do more about career planning?	

Name _____ **Date** _____

TENTATIVE CAREER PLAN WORKSHEET

Directions: Fill in the activities you have experienced or plan to experience that contribute to your career planning process.

CAREER GOAL

_____

_____

_____

_____

AWARENESS includes self-knowledge and an understanding of the world of work, with the ability to see connections between the two in making career choices.

_____

_____

_____

_____

EXPLORATION includes the opportunities to investigate careers through information resources and hands-on experiences.

_____

_____

_____

_____

PLANNING includes a sequence of steps that leads to career training and placement.

_____

_____

_____

_____

CRITIQUING YOUR RESPONSES TO "MY PERSONAL CAREER PLAN" IN THE *GET A LIFE* PORTFOLIO

Directions: Read "My Personal Career Plan" in the *Get a Life* portfolio. Ask yourself these questions:

• What can be answered?

_____

_____

_____

• What questions need more research?

_____

_____

_____

• What other information do I need?

_____

_____

_____

• What do I need to do to get the information?

_____

_____

_____

• Who can help me?

_____

_____

_____

• What other resources can I use to complete my plan?

_____

_____

_____

OBJECTIVES:

1. Students will know the sequence of the career planning process.

2. Students will evaluate their progress in the career planning process.

3. Students will be able to generate personal strategies for revising their career plans, as needed.

SUPPLIES:

"Come to Order" worksheet

PORTFOLIO ENTRY: *Career Exploration and Planning,* Competency Skills, *"Applies Decision Making"*

COME TO ORDER
Career Exploration and Planning
"Career Planning Process"

LESSON	NOTES
1. **Introduction:** Remind students that choosing a career is a process and not a one-step choice. Discuss the meaning of "process."	
2. **Focus:** In pairs, ask students to sequence the career planning process on the worksheet. Student answers may differ. After ample time is given, discuss the differences in the sequencing and the reasons for them.	
3. **Activity:** Have each student evaluate the status of his or her career process. In the large group, have students discuss the activities they have done in school to support each step. Then ask students where the activities are lacking. Generate possible activities that will help to complete the process.	
4. **Closure:** Ask: Why is sequencing in the career process important? What or who can help you in this process? What did you learn about career decision making?	
5. **Follow-up:** Ask students to commit to a goal to complete one activity that will further their career process. Assess goals in a reasonable amount of time.	

COME TO ORDER WORKSHEET

Directions: Number each step in the career process from beginning to completion, and give reasons for the placement.

_____ MAKE A TENTATIVE DECISION

_____

_____

_____ COMPARE AND WEIGH THE INFORMATION

_____

_____

_____ EVALUATE THE PROGRESS

_____

_____

_____ GATHER INFORMATION

_____

_____

_____ IMPLEMENT THE PLAN

_____

_____

_____ STUDY YOURSELF

_____

_____

_____ EXPLORE ALTERNATIVES

_____

_____

COME TO ORDER WORKSHEET

Directions: Number each step in the career process from beginning to completion, and give reasons for the placement.

_6_   MAKE A TENTATIVE DECISION

This is the hard part, but it's easier if you did all the other steps first.

_4_   COMPARE AND WEIGH THE INFORMATION

List the pros and cons of each.

_5_   EVALUATE THE PROGRESS

Pause to clear your head and think about all that you've accomplished and all that you still need to do.

_2_   GATHER INFORMATION

Collect all you can about all possible career choices.

_7_   IMPLEMENT THE PLAN

Now, do it! Remember, you can change your mind but this step gives you a sense of accomplishment.

_1_   STUDY YOURSELF

Understand that a career choice is personally suited to you. You have to know what you like and what you do well.

_3_   EXPLORE ALTERNATIVES

Ask others if you've covered all the possibilities, then explore new ones. Think about what might happen if you do make any one of the choices.

OBJECTIVES:

1. Students will be able to develop an outline that helps them target pertinent information for a personal career search.

2. Students will be able to investigate two occupations of interest using vocational information resources.

3. Students will be able to report their occupational interest findings.

SUPPLIES:

Career resources (ask the school counselor for some of these)

Chart paper

PORTFOLIO ENTRY: *Career Exploration and Planning,* Competency Skills, *"Career Information"*

PRIVATE "I"

Career Exploration and Planning

"Using Career Information"

LESSON	NOTES
1. **Introduction:** Tell students that they will be "private investigators" for two particular career choices. (These jobs may be selected by the student, assigned by the teacher, or picked at random.)	
2. **Focus:** Tell students that in order to have an orderly research of a career, they must agree on certain areas of investigation.	
3. **Activity:** Ask students what they would like to know about a potential career choice. Chart answers. (Examples: job description, salary range, training needed, etc.) Create a collective outline and duplicate for each class member. Allow students ample time to research each of two occupations, using available career resources.	
4. **Closure:** Ask: What did you learn from this lesson? What other jobs would you like to research? Which is your favorite resource? Post reports and allow students time to read them.	
5. **Follow-up:** Encourage students to share their reports with parents.	

OBJECTIVES:

1. Students will be able to complete a career assessment inventory.

2. Students will be able to understand the results of the assessment.

3. Students will be able to synthesize and enter the information learned from the assessment into a career portfolio.

SUPPLIES:

Career assessment tool (e.g., interest inventory, aptitude test, personality assessment, etc.)

NOTE: If your school does not have any career assessments, contact a Career Development or Counselor Education program at a local university for information about titles and ordering.

PORTFOLIO ENTRY: *Career Exploration and Planning, Results of Career Assessment*

COLLECTING INTEREST
Career Exploration and Planning
"Using Career Information"

LESSON	NOTES
1. **Introduction:** Tell students that they will be using an assessment tool that will give them useful information for making career decisions.	
2. **Focus:** Use the reference material that accompanies the assessment tool to prepare students for this activity.	
3. **Activity:** Give ample time for students to complete the assessment tool. (The time may vary from student to student.) When assessment tools have been scored, continue the lesson. Give students appropriate materials that will allow them to understand and interpret the scores.* When appropriate, give **bring** oral review of interpretation information using overheads or diagrams provided in assessment manuals. Encourage small and large group discussion about the scoring results. Then have students enter appropriate information in a career portfolio (e.g., *Get a Life*).	
4. **Closure:** Ask: How can the assessment tool we used be useful to your career plans? What information did you gain from this tool? What other assessment tools would assist your career planning? What other information do you need to know about yourself to assist you in making career decisions?	
5. **Follow-up:** Assist students in taking additional assessment tools if requested.	

*It is important for students to hear that assessments only *suggest* possible career options—they don't tell students what they should choose.

OBJECTIVES:

1. Students will be able to identify and assess personal work experience.

2. Students will be able to compare personal work experience with an objective assessment tool.

3. Students will be able to draw conclusions from this comparison that relate to the career planning process.

SUPPLIES:

"Collecting More Interest" worksheet

Previously administered assessment tool (See "Collecting Interest.")

PORTFOLIO ENTRY: *Career Exploration and Planning, Results of Career Assessment*

COLLECTING MORE INTEREST

Career Exploration and Planning

"Using Career Information"

LESSON	NOTES
1. **Introduction:** Tell students that they will be assessing their own personal work experience as it relates to the career planning process.	
2. **Focus:** Ask students to brainstorm all volunteer and paid positions they have held during their school years (Examples: babysitting, scouting, clerk, food vendor). Have students list them in Part I of the worksheet.	
3. **Activity:** Discuss Part II of the worksheet. In pairs, have students categorize their work experience and note insights. (Give ample time for reflection.) Distribute previously administered individual assessment tools that have already been scored. Give ample time for students to compare their subjective work insights with the objective assessment tool. Have students make generalizations and draw conclusions.	
4. **Closure:** Ask: What did you learn from this lesson? How will it assist you in choosing a career? What additional information is necessary?	

COLLECTING MORE INTEREST WORKSHEET

Part I

Directions: List all work experience, volunteer or paid, that you have had during your school years.

_____   _____

_____   _____

_____   _____

_____   _____

- -

Part II

Directions: Place each work experience into one or more categories below and make brief notes on each.

Job skills (Example: Hospital volunteer—serve food trays, pick up trays, answer call bells, assist nurse.)

_____

_____

_____

People skills (Example: Hospital volunteer—must be flexible working with sick people, follow orders, listening skills.)

_____

_____

_____

Personal insights (Example: Hospital volunteer—too depressing, but enjoy working with people.)

_____

_____

_____

Sample student responses to worksheet

COLLECTING MORE INTEREST WORKSHEET

Part I

lawn mowing
dog care
walk-a-thon participant
10th grade class vice president
band, grades 6-12
senior lifesaving
lifeguard

Part II

Job Skills

lawn mowing—cut, rake, trim
dog care—feed, walk, groom
lifeguard—responsible for safety of beachgoers

People Skills

10th grade vice president—represent students in school government

Personal Skills

Walk-a-thon—fund raising for charity
band—develop leisure time activity
senior lifesaving—preparing for job skill

NICE ATTITUDE
Career Exploration and Planning
"Positive Work Attitudes"

OBJECTIVES:

1. Students will be able to conduct interviews on the definition of "work ethic."

2. Students will be able to draw conclusions from the variety of responses.

3. Students will be able to select definitions they agree upon, and report the results to the interviewees.

SUPPLIES:

"Nice Attitude Interview Rules" worksheet

"Nice Attitude Interview" worksheet

Chart paper

Markers

NICE ATTITUDE
Career Exploration and Planning
"Positive Work Attitudes"

LESSON	NOTES
1. **Introduction:** Tell students that they will be collecting "work ethic" information through interviews.	

2. **Focus:** Instruct students in appropriate methods of interviewing. (See "Nice Attitude Interview Rules" sheets and discuss.)

3. **Activity:** Discuss and define the meaning of work ethic. Ask students to interview 10 adults using the "Nice Attitude Interview" worksheet. Give ample time for completing (2-5 days). In class, ask students to share and chart the responses and combine those that are similar. Have students discuss in small groups, and choose their personal two or three favorite choices. Have students share their small group choices in the large group and give reasons for their selections. When discussion is completed, ask students to commit to sharing the results with the people they interviewed. Have a follow-up discussion with those who completed this task.

4. **Closure:** Ask: How difficult is it to interview? Was the interview model a type of work ethic? How can you improve the next time you interview? Why is a work ethic important? How will your idea of a work ethic change as you get more job experience? How will this experience contribute to your job experience?

NICE ATTITUDE INTERVIEW RULES

1. Make contact—phone or contact in person.

2. Explain project—tell the person that you will be asking them and nine others to define "work ethic" for a career awareness lesson. Also tell interviewees that you will be recording or taking notes.

3. Set a time and date—give the person a few options for convenience.

4. Keep appointment—arrive on time and be prepared with a tape recorder or writing tools.

5. Conduct the interview.

6. Thank interviewee—thank the people for spending the time with you and tell them you will report the results if they'd like to know them.

NOTES:

_____

_____

_____

_____

_____

_____

_____

_____

_____

Student Name _____ **Date** _____

NICE ATTITUDE INTERVIEW SHEET
(Reproduce if more sheets are needed.)

Directions: Ask: What is your definition of the term "work ethic"?

Name: _____

Response and comments:

_____

_____

_____

_____

Name: _____

Response and comments:

_____

_____

_____

_____

Name: _____

Response and comments:

_____

_____

_____

_____

Name: _____

Response and comments:

_____

_____

_____

_____

POSITIVE REFLECTIONS
Career Exploration and Planning
"Positive Work Attitudes"

OBJECTIVES:

1. Students will be able to define the term "attitude."

2. Students will be able to identify the effects of attitude on work behavior and performance.

3. Students will be able to draw conclusions about the relationship between self-concept and work attitude.

SUPPLIES:

Dictionary

PORTFOLIO ENTRY: *Career Exploration and Planning,* My Personal Career Plan, *Job-Seeking Skills*

POSITIVE REFLECTIONS
Career Exploration and Planning
"Positive Work Attitudes"

LESSON	NOTES

1. **Introduction:** Tell students they will be investigating how attitudes about work affect job behavior and performance.

2. **Focus:** Ask students to define "attitude" and give examples of it as it relates to work performance.

3. **Activity:** Have students define "self-concept." In small groups, discuss the relationship between self-concept and work attitude (Example: pride/lack of pride in finished product). Share conclusions in large group.

4. **Closure:** Ask: What did you learn about the relationships between self-concept and work attitude? How can workers change their own attitudes? How important is the employer in changing attitudes?

5. **Follow-up:** Have students share personal experiences in this area. See next lesson, "Positive Press."

OBJECTIVES:

1. Students will be able to interview employers about the work attitudes they desire in an employee.

2. Students will be able to draw conclusions from these interviews.

3. Students will be able to publish a newspaper piece about work attitudes.

SUPPLIES:

List of community employers

PORTFOLIO ENTRY: *Career Exploration and Planning, Results of Career Assessment, Pre-Employment Experiences, or* My Personal Career Plan, *"Career Exploration"*

POSITIVE PRESS

Career Exploration and Planning

"Positive Work Attitudes"

LESSON	NOTES
1. **Introduction:** Tell students that they will be investigating the importance of work attitudes from the perspective of the employer.	
2. **Focus:** Review the rules of interviewing (See "Nice Attitude" lesson on page 200.)	
3. **Activity:** Assign students three employers (or have them suggest ones) to interview on the question, "Which three to five work attitudes do you consider important for an employee to possess?" Give ample time (3-5 days) for the students to gather the information. In small group, discuss the findings and consolidate the information into five to eight categories. Report to the large group. Ask students to reassemble into groups of three and write a collaborative news article addressing the topic of work attitude. Submit articles to the school newspaper.	
4. **Closure:** Ask: What did you learn from this activity? Which employee attitudes did local employers hold in common? Do you think that in a setting different from your community, these attitudes would be similar? How will what you learned affect your attitude in a job interview or on the job?	
5. **Follow-up:** Submit the articles to a local newspaper or teen magazine.	

OBJECTIVES:

1. Students will be able to identify five possible career choices.

2. Students will be able to use personal criteria to prioritize the choices, using a scale.

3. Students will be able to defend their highest-ranking choices based on personal experience.

SUPPLIES:

"Preferential Treatment" worksheet

PORTFOLIO ENTRY: *Career Exploration and Planning,* My Personal Career Plan, *"Career Options"*

PREFERENTIAL TREATMENT

Career Exploration and Planning

"Career Decisions"

LESSON	NOTES
1. **Introduction:** Tell students that they will be applying the decision-making process as it relates to choosing a career.	
2. **Focus:** Ask students to enumerate five viable career choices. Discuss when and why they thought of the careers selected.	
3. **Activity:** Discuss the items on the "Preferential Treatment" worksheet as they relate to the students' individual aptitudes, interests, category preferences (data, people, things, ideas), etc. Have students rank each item for each career choice and total each column. In small groups, have students explain their highest-ranking career possibilities.	
4. **Closure:** Ask: What did you learn from this lesson? How will it help you in the future? Why is career decision making important to investigate?	
5. **Follow-up:** Have students share the results with a best friend and ask for feedback. Also see the "Public Defending" lesson on page 216.	

Name _____ Date _____

PREFERENTIAL TREATMENT WORKSHEET

Directions: Place five viable career choices in the TITLE boxes. Rank each career choice according to how well each provides opportunities for personal expression.

4—very satisfying   3—fair   2—tolerable   1—no way

TITLE	1:	2:	3:	4:	5:
Personal strengths					
Educational aptitude					
Interests					
Category preference (data, ideas, people, things)					
Personality					
Work value					
Other					
TOTAL SCORE					

Sample Student Worksheet

PREFERENTIAL TREATMENT WORKSHEET

Directions: Place five viable career choices in the TITLE boxes. Rank each career choice according to how well each provides opportunities for personal expression.

4—very satisfying   3—fair   2—tolerable   1—no way

TITLE	1: Graphic Artist	2: Landscape Gardener	3: Chef	4: Prepress Worker	5: Drafter
Personal strengths	4	4	3	2	3
Educational aptitude	3	3	4	2	3
Interests	4	4	3	2	4
Category preference (data, ideas, people, things)	4	3	3	2	4
Personality	3	3	3	3	2
Work value	4	4	3	2	4
Other	3	3	3	3	2
TOTAL SCORE	25	24	22	16	22

FRIENDLY ADVICE
Career Exploration and Planning
"Career Decisions"

OBJECTIVES:

1. Students will be able to identify the steps necessary for becoming a responsible career decision maker.

2. Students will be able to generate answers to questions about facilitating career decision making.

3. Students will be able to evaluate their support roles in the career decision-making process of another.

SUPPLIES:

Chart paper

Markers

"Friendly Advice" worksheet

PORTFOLIO ENTRY: *Career Exploration and Planning,* My Personal Career Plan, *"Career Plan"*

FRIENDLY ADVICE
Career Exploration and Planning
"Career Decisions"

LESSON	NOTES
1. **Introduction:** Ask students to think of the person in their lives who is most important to them at this moment. Ask for examples.	
2. **Focus:** Tell them to pretend that this person has come to them for help in listing the steps they must take to make a successful career decision.	
3. **Activity:** Individually, have students list the steps. Chart the steps for review. Have students answer the questions on the "Friendly Advice" worksheet. (Students may work in pairs to help each other.)	
4. **Closure:** Ask: How can this lesson help you with future career decisions? What roles do friends play in your career decision making? What important messages should you keep in mind when advising friends about career decisions?	

FRIENDLY ADVICE WORKSHEET

Directions: Answer the following questions as if you were advising an important friend about his or her career.

Who would you recommend this person talk with other than yourself?

_____

_____

_____

How can you judge where this person is in his/her career decision-making process?

_____

_____

_____

What resources would you recommend to help this individual?

_____

_____

_____

What are some possible stumbling blocks that might interfere with your being able to help this person?

_____

_____

_____

FRIENDLY ADVICE WORKSHEET

Directions: Answer the following questions as if you were advising an important friend about his or her career.

Who would you recommend this person talk with other than yourself?

The stepfather—who is doing what she would like to do. She likes him and respects his opinion.

How can you judge where this person is in his/her career decision-making process?

She is ready to select courses to study, so I think she's in the planning stage, but she is still exploring.

What resources would you recommend to help this individual?

Go to an advisor at the state college to plan a course of study.

What are some possible stumbling blocks that might interfere with your being able to help this person?

I'm going to a two-year technology school, so I don't know some of the things she needs to look into at a four-year school. Besides, I'm just a friend, not a professional.

A STEP IN TIME
Career Exploration and Planning
"Career Decisions"

OBJECTIVES:

1. Students will be able to recall the major steps in the career decision-making process.

2. Students will be able to identify where they are in the process.

3. Students will be able to plan their next steps in the process, and set goals and timelines for completion.

SUPPLIES:

Chart paper

Markers

PORTFOLIO ENTRY: *Career Exploration and Planning,* My Personal Career Plan, *"Career Decision"*

A STEP IN TIME

Career Exploration and Planning

"Career Decisions"

LESSON	NOTES
1. **Introduction:** Review the "Friendly Advice" lesson on page 211.	
2. **Focus:** Tell students that now it is time to apply those same steps in a personal way to their own career decisions.	
3. **Activity:** In small groups, have students identify which step they are at in the career decision-making process. Ask them to identify activities that they did to support each previous level. Enter the information in a career portfolio (e.g., *Get a Life*). Individually, students should be able to predict the next step to be taken and the time line for that step. Discuss in pairs. In large group, chart individuals' next steps and the expected time lines for completion of those steps.	
4. **Closure:** Ask: Why is decision making so difficult? Is it important to set goals and time lines? Why? What happens when a goal is not met? How important is it to monitor your progress in meeting major life goals?	
5. **Follow-up:** Check on progress in a month.	

OBJECTIVES:

1. Students will be able to list job opportunities for students who cannot apply for a work permit.

2. Students will be able to list the employment skills gained by having these positions.

3. Students will be able to analyze how the attainment of these skills will contribute to future employment.

SUPPLIES:

Chart paper

Markers

PORTFOLIO ENTRY: *Career Exploration and Planning,* My Personal Career Plan, *"Linking Self-Knowledge"*

WORK STUDY

Career Exploration and Planning

"Job-Seeking Skills"

LESSON	NOTES
1. **Introduction:** Tell students that this lesson will concentrate on how students of their age make money today.	
2. **Focus:** Have students brainstorm in large group all the jobs they can have without a work permit (e.g., babysitting, lawn mowing, paper delivering, etc.).	
3. **Activity:** In small groups, ask students to list and analyze all the job skills developed by each position. Examples might include: child-care skills, scheduling, phone skills, physical stamina, advertising, money management, etc. Discuss future occupations that utilize the same skills.	
4. **Closure:** Ask: What did you learn from this lesson? How will present jobs affect future employment? Should students your age have jobs?	
5. **Follow-up:** Survey the class to determine the number of students who have jobs. Have them suggest methods of attaining jobs for the "unemployed" classmates.	

TO SUM THINGS UP
Career Exploration and Planning
"Job-Seeking Skills"

OBJECTIVES:

1. Students will be able to list the key points to include in a one-page personal resume.

2. Students will be able to rewrite a resume including their own suggestions for improvement.

3. Students will be able to critique and offer suggestions to improve classmates' resumes.

SUPPLIES:

Resume examples

Chart paper

Markers

PORTFOLIO ENTRY: *Career Exploration and Planning,* My Personal Career Plan, *Job Seeking Skills*

218

Career Exploration and Planning

"Job-Seeking Skills"

LESSON	NOTES
1. **Introduction:** Tell students that this lesson will allow them to make an investment in their futures.	
2. **Focus:** Ask them how employers pre-screen interviewees (Examples: phone call, resume, references, etc.).	
3. **Activity:** In small groups, have students brainstorm the key points they would include on a personal resume. (Examples: skills developed in school, decision-making ability, awards, recognitions, etc.). Share lists in larger group and chart the ideas. Pass out the resume examples. Individually, have students read a resume and add or edit the piece based on the suggestions from their brainstormed list. Discuss in small groups and report out in the large group. (Are they aware that employers *cannot* ask for certain information?)	
4. **Closure:** Ask: How would you rank the original resumes: fair, good, excellent? Would you interview a candidate based on the first resume? the improved one? How will this lesson contribute to your future job prospects?	
5. **Follow-up:** Have students write personal resumes using the improved samples as a guide. Ask classmates to critique them. Put in final copy.	

RESUME (VITA)

Name: Kim Etudiante

Address: 123 School Street
                  Townshire, USA

Telephone: (555) 555-1234

Date of Birth: 2/14/80

Marital Status: Single

Particulars: Height 5'8" Weight 150

Education: Townshire High School
                  Vocational Tech-Prep
                  anticipated graduation date 6/98

Salary Desired: negotiable

Experience: 1994-present   Summer Counselor-in-Training
                                  Camp Get-a-Life
                                  Got-one USA
                  1993-1994   Phar-Out Drug Store
                                  part-time delivery, weekends
                  1990-1993   Babysitting duties
                                  summers and weekends

References: Mr. Bud Plante, Guidance Director
                  Townshire High School
                  Townshire, USA 12345

                  Mrs. Jack Enjill
                  Waterhill Road
                  Tumbleweed, USA 23456

                  Dr. Al Gebra
                  2345 N.W. 18th Street
                  Mathematica, USA

RESUME (VITA) (Continued)

Terry Schoolsmart
234 School Street
Bright City, USA 99990
(555) 555-4321

Education:	Bright City High School Vocational Tech-Prep Anticipated graduation in clerical science, 6/99

Experience:

1994-present	Summer camp experiences
1995-present	Substitute office helper on weekends at a local health food store
1995-present	Lighting director for productions in the high school auditorium

Competencies: Coursework has included word processing, basic accounting, spreadsheets, data bases, and Internet applications

I got an award for a project in my word processing class

References: Mrs. Paul
(One of the camp counselors)

Mr. H. Gilmore
(Boss at my weekend job)

Ms. Whoozonphirst
(Coach)

OBJECTIVES:

1. Students will be able to analyze the interview process from a videotaped example.

2. Students will be able to develop and refine a list of interview questions.

3. Students will be able to create a role play, conduct it, and analyze it from the viewpoint of both the interviewer and the interviewee.

SUPPLIES:

Mock interview on videotape (Contact local career center or have drama students create one.)

Chart paper

Markers

PORTFOLIO ENTRY: *Career Exploration and Planning,* My Personal Career Plan, *Job-Seeking Skills*

INNER-VIEW
Career Exploration and Planning
"Job-Seeking Skills"

LESSON	NOTES
1. **Introduction:** Tell students that they will be analyzing an interview. Ask them to note what happens, what is asked, and what resulted from the interchange.	
2. **Focus:** View the videotape, stopping periodically for students to take notes.	
3. **Activity:** Ask students about the format of the interview. Outline the format on chart paper. (Example: greeting, light conversation, information given, salary discussed, etc.). List the questions asked. Have students add to or edit the questions asked in the video. In small group, have students create a role play interview. Give sufficient time for planning. Perform the role plays for the large group and chart the information given by the interviewee and by the interviewer. Analyze the interchange.	
4. **Closure:** Ask: What did you learn from this lesson? How will it help you during the interview process? How "real" is a role play?	
5. **Follow-up:** Have students who are going to be interviewed for real-life jobs brainstorm possible questions that might be asked. Discuss relaxation and stress reduction techniques.	

EPILOGUE

A Look in the Rearview Mirror

Reflections on *Lessons for Life*

An educator who practices the art of "reflective learning" looks back on a lesson and examines how things went and how things could be improved. Furthermore, the reflective learner seeks insight from the lessons that will nurture future growth within the profession. The attached evaluation sheets are offered as resources to help in this reflective process. You will need to make multiple copies so that you can evaluate individual lessons and assess student receptivity to both the activities and the objectives. While there is much more to reflection than student and self-evaluation, you are encouraged to use these evaluations as two sets of information that can be used for program reflection and refinement.

As we reflect on the experience of creating these *Lessons for Life,* we are excited about the opportunities that students will have for analyzing, synthesizing, and evaluating the various facets of their career development. As we have talked with educators and shared some of the lessons, we have repeatedly heard the message, "I wish I had had some experiences like these when I was in school!" As a part of our own learning process, we have found personal meaning in many of these lessons because we, too, are lifelong learners who are constantly making meaning of our own career journeys. If life is a journey, we hope we have provided some of the pages of the atlas, as well as some insights about how to enjoy the trip.

FACILITATOR'S EVALUATION SHEET

Lesson Title: _____ Level: _____

Were the objectives met?   ☐ Yes   ☐ No

Were supplies adequate?   ☐ Yes   ☐ No

The best part of the lesson/unit was:

_____

_____

_____

Suggestions to improve the lesson are: _____

_____

_____

_____

Here's what I learned about myself as an instructor/learner: _____

_____

_____

_____

Comments: _____

_____

_____

_____

STUDENT EVALUATION SHEET

Lesson Title: _____ Level: _____

This lesson taught me: _____

_____

_____

_____

The best part of this lesson was: _____

_____

_____

_____

Suggestions to improve this lesson are: _____

_____

_____

_____

Here's what I learned about myself: _____

_____

_____

_____

Comments: _____

_____

_____

_____

NOTES

NOTES

NOTES

NOTES

NOTES

NOTES

NOTES

NOTES

NOTES

NOTES

NOTES

NOTES

NOTES